Dirt Roads to Dixie

*Accessibility and Modernization
in the South, 1885–1935*

Howard Lawrence Preston

The University of Tennessee Press
Knoxville

Copyright © 1991 by The University of Tennessee Press / Knoxville.
All Rights Reserved. Manufactured in the United States of America.
First Edition.

Frontispiece: Road Marker, Crossville, Tennessee ca. 1937.
Courtesy of the Library of Congress.

The paper in this book meets the minimum requirements of the
American National Standard for Permanence of Paper for Printed
Library Materials. ⊚ The binding materials have been chosen for
strength and durability.

Library of Congress Cataloging in Publication Data

Preston, Howard L.
  Dirt roads to Dixie : accessibility and modernization in the
South, 1885–1935 / Howard Lawrence Preston. – 1st ed.
      p.   cm.
  Includes bibliographical references.
  ISBN 0-87049-676-X (cloth: alk. paper)
  ISBN 0-87049-677-8 (pbk.: alk paper)
    1. Rural roads–Southern States–History. 2. Roads–Southern
States–History. I. Title.
HE336.R85P74 1991
388.1'0975'09034–dc20   90-37726 CIP

For Jay and Elizabeth

Contents

Illustrations

Figures

Dirt Roads to Dixie

Introduction

Today a person can be born, bred, and buried in the South without ever realizing that this place is, and has been, significantly different from the rest of the nation. Without question, the region still remains culturally distinct. A more relaxed way of life, southerners' slower patterns of speech, the preponderance of religious fundamentalism, and the widely held notion that good manners are an expression of social morality, among many other cultural characteristics, continue to distinguish the South and its people. But much has also changed. And in this century, as Dixie has begun to disappear, it has done so first along the highway where twentieth-century modernization in the form of chain stores, fast-food restaurants, gasoline stations, and motels—all geared to accommodating a faster-paced nation constantly on the move—is replacing the region's cultural identity with a wholesale, predictable sameness.

I grew up in the South and, except for a two-year hitch in the military, have never lived or worked elsewhere. Some would call that the essence of provincialism, but I prefer the region to any other part of the country because I recognize its historical uniqueness and bemoan the plastic, predictable culture that is replacing it. Although I am unable to pinpoint exactly when I became aware that there was such a place as "the South," I can recall one occasion when I realized that the region I called home was, at least, different. I was twelve, a city boy, schooled in the convictions of good taste and the proper social graces. That summer of my twelfth year, my maternal grandmother, whom I called "Nomie," and I departed our hometown of Atlanta for a much-anticipated Florida vacation. The name I gave my grandmother resulted from the long-entrenched southern custom of respect for one's elders. I had heard my mother say "No'm" to her, for "No, Ma'am," so often that I grew up thinking her name was "Nomie." As we drove south in her '53 Ford coupe to meet the rest of my family, who had departed by train a few days earlier, Nomie made the point that we could stay on the Dixie Highway (U.S. 41) all the way to Florida.

We drove part of the morning and all afternoon, and just before nightfall, somewhere south of Valdosta, Nomie decided that she had driven enough for one day and advised me to look for a suitable place to spend the night. I, of course, assumed she meant a motel. But to her, motels, or tourist cottages as she called them, were for motorized gypsies and automobile hobos, certainly not places that accommodated people with high standards of southern civility. What she meant for me to be on the lookout for was a tourist home, a clean room in someone's private residence maintained in a way any self-respecting southern woman cared for the rest of her house. I remember passing the flickering neon lights of several motels before we found what my grandmother had in mind: a house set some distance from the highway under a canopy of spreading live oak trees. To my chagrin, Nomie insisted on a room with a private bath, so that I might bathe before going to bed. I failed to understand how a person could get all that dirty riding in a car, and to this day I can vividly recall climbing into a bathtub of the most nauseous-smelling sulfur water imaginable and holding my nose while I washed. After promising myself that I would never take another bath, I hopped into a bed with a lumpy mattress and fell asleep listening to a chorus of crickets in the trees outside the open window.

That childhood experience was only a generation ago, and I regret that my children, who are so accustomed to a roadside culture of McDonald's restaurants and Holiday Inn motels, will never know that traveling by automobile in the South was once a real adventure. Roads like the Dixie Highway or the Robert E. Lee Highway and overnight accommodations in southerners' homes gave automobile trips a certain fortuity; and of course, it was never a foregone conclusion that motorists could make their destination in an allotted time.

During the twentieth century, motoring below the Mason-Dixon line has gone from next to impossible to an anticipated ease. Trips that once took days, and even weeks, now take only a matter of hours; and it is possible to travel the full breadth of the region on a highway as culturally bland in Georgia as in New Jersey. The early automobile age and the national Progressive Era, a period in American history that saw unprecedented social and political change occur throughout the country, coincided. How did the new automobile technology and this ethos of reform that consumed Americans help make the South more like the rest of the nation? What role did southerners play in this process of change? And what kind of South emerged as a result? To provide an answer to these and other questions important to understanding the evolution of the modern twentieth-century South, I have organized the seven chapters of this book into two parts. Part One is about the good roads movement, a cause which historian Francis B. Simkins called "the third god [along with education and industrial development] in the Trinity of southern progress."[1] Because its proponents argued tirelessly and relentlessly that improved roads were the best way to accomplish needed changes in the South, the issue of good roads attracted the attention of countless southerners. The good roads movement was one of the least controversial reform campaigns in the region's history and has been identified as one of the popular causes in the South during the early decades of the twentieth century deserving of the label "progressive." In Part Two I have assessed the results of good roads progressivism and have attempted to determine whether its proponents actually accomplished any of their objectives.

In chapter one I describe what the improvement of the South's public roads meant to late nineteenth and early twentieth century southerners. These reforms promised to remake the region into a more humane and desirable place in which to live. Rural life would be enhanced, and farmers would become more prosperous.

In chapters two and three, I show how another generation of southerners who defined "progress" in different terms deliberately altered the original reform objectives of the good roads movement to accommodate automobile tourism, and by focusing on John Asa Rountree, one of the most visible proponents of road improvements in the South during the early twentieth century, I reveal the extent to which good roads progressivism strayed from its original purposes. Clearly, when it came to the good roads movement, there was little, if any, reconciliation between progressive reform and the quest for post–Civil War economic development that Professor Dewey Grantham has found in other progressive campaigns at this time in the South.

Thus I have put the good roads movement in a perspective that is at once contradictory to what has been called Progressivism both in the South and elsewhere. Certainly the South shared in the progressive spirit of the nation, experienced similar reform impulses, and as Grantham has noted, "interacted with other parts of the country in developing its own brand of progressivism."[2] But progress to rank-and-file southerners, who liked to think of themselves as wanting to build a better future for the South, did not mean the same thing to New Englanders or midwesterners. Consequently, there has always been a question of whether the reform notions of southerners during the early part of the twentieth century were in the same league as national Progressivism. The point has been well made that in the South economic development stood for progress more than anything else, and any and all other reform tendencies that can be labeled "progressive" followed. My intention here is to expound upon this theme, not belabor it, and to shed greater light on how one of the curious activities that passed for progressivism – the good roads movement – had little meaning in the South in terms of actual reforms.

The issue of good roads, as we shall see, was one on which the success of many progressive ideals in the South hinged. But unlike other reform movements at this same time, the original objectives of southerners who wanted to help farmers by improving road conditions – and thereby offer a better standard of living to all rural southerners – were easily corrupted. Because of the very real and immediate prospect of attracting automobile tourists from other parts of the country, business-minded southerners were able to transform the good roads movement from an effort to construct rural farm-to-market roads into a well-funded, highly visible, and sustained effort to build tourist highways.

To those who identified in some way with the notion of the New South – the well-publicized concept that the region had an unlimited potential for economic opportunity, an uncommon atmosphere for investment opportunity, and a fervid climate for business intensified by a public-spirited enthusiasm – these highways were the very symbols of progress. They were to the rural South what skyscrapers were to the urban South: an undeniable sign of economic vitality, tangible evidence that the inferior South was finally exchanging its backwardness for progress, and a manifestation of a region that was no longer stagnant but vibrant and on the move. By the time the nation elected Woodrow Wilson to his second White House term, men and women who subscribed to the ideal of a New South – namely middle-class executives, politicians, and land developers – had discarded the reform goals of good roads progressivism and replaced them with objectives of their own. To this group, signs of wealth and commercial and industrial achievement, and not the accessibility of farmers to markets, gave progress its meaning. Once this happened, good roads lost their significance as a reform issue.

Business leaders, the new advocates for the good roads movement in the South – those like Rountree who have been mistakenly included in the group that sought grassroots changes for the South – were, in fact, wolves in sheep's clothing. They abandoned the populist notions of the good roads movement in favor of their own wallets. Interstate highways like the Dixie Highway, the Lee Highway, the Jefferson Davis Highway, and the Bankhead National Highway promised to bring in tourist dollars and vital new industries as well as generate a never before realized potential for economic prosperity. These were the very goals of the "New South," and as a result, many southerners began to view interstate tourist highways and the realization of their ambitions for prosperity as inseparable. Those who advocated the construction of routes that extended into other parts of the United States, therefore, deserve to be distinguished from other southern progressives who were not as profit-minded. Throughout the book, therefore, I have chosen to identify this second contingent of good roads advocates in the South as "highway progressives."

There were, then, two groups of southerners who called themselves good roads progressives: the original faction of disgruntled turn-of-the-century farmers and intellectuals who perceived road improvements as a panacea for improving the downtrodden, rural, impoverished South and as means of restoring a measure of the agrarian values that were losing importance in an increasingly urban-industrial society; and a subsequently formed second group, "highway progressives," who espoused all the rhetoric of the first contingent of good roads reformers but who had at heart the motivations of capitalists. If the members of the first group, who were dissatisfied with rural life in the South and sought a means by which to improve it, had been able to construct their once-envisioned network of local roads connecting isolated hamlets throughout the region with larger towns and market centers, then the twentieth-century rural South would not have been so chronically backward.

Highway progressives were much more businesslike in their approach to road improvements, and the only common thread between their development programs and other reform efforts underway in the South at the same time was that material progress in the form of economic development, if indeed that can be construed to be progressivism, was an objective. Thus, if the implicit goal of southern progressives, as Grantham has written, was the creation of a more unified, cohesive, humane, orderly, efficient, and (with blacks excluded) democratic South, then the good roads movement as a manifestation of that progressive spirit certainly missed its mark.

Thinking about southern progressivism is in some ways like broaching the subject of urbanization. Generalizations can be made, but to say that one city developed the same way as another is pre-

mature without careful examination of each. We will never actually know how "progressive" Progressivism was in the South or
how it compares to reform campaigns outside the region until his-
torians roll up their sleeves and delve into the many reform activities labeled "progressive." The first part of this book, then, is
a step in that direction.

The effect of highway progressivism in the South, or to put it
another way, what was achieved by the construction of long-distance
interstate highways that connected the South with other parts of
the nation, is a concern of the second part of the volume. In chapter four I tell the story of an automobile trip made by an adventurous Connecticut Yankee from his home state to faraway Charleston, South Carolina. The year was 1910, a time when automobile
technology was as primitive as the roads over which motorists traveled. Simply from the list of necessary equipment that this fearless
New Englander carried with him in his sturdy touring car, it is
not difficult to see how remote and isolated the region was from
the rest of the nation at that not-so-long-ago date. In chapter five
I account for the hegira of automobile tourism that highway progressivism, together with the popular romantic notion many Americans had of the South, generated.

Finally, I have documented what began to happen to the South
in the wake of this unprecedented wave of tourism and how the
widespread ownership of automobiles on the part of southerners,
and not progressive reform, is what really made the original objective of good roads progressivism in the South—improved local
roads—a reality. More than thirty years after southerners sounded
the call for road improvements as a solution to the South's woes,
little had changed. Backwardness in education, commerce, and industry still characterized the region better than advancements in
these important areas. But interstate highway construction and the
widespread ownership of automobiles in the South did generate
change. Southerners' newfound automobility and improved, well-
publicized tourists routes were catalysts for nationalism below the
Mason-Dixon line. Interstate highways opened the region for the
first time to the rest of the nation and introduced southerners to

a new national popular culture manifest in filling stations, tourist cabins, endless roadside advertising, autocamps, tin-can tourists, and a variety of automobile-related businesses that accelerated the South toward modernization and helped Americans awaken to view the region as a leisure-time paradise. The good roads movement, therefore, may have failed to change the South the way that those who saw road improvements as progressive reforms first envisioned. But this brand of southern progressivism – highway progressivism – did begin a process of change that ultimately challenged the region's provinciality and eventually led to a more modern South whose residents conformed to national as well as regional cultural standards.

My sincere thanks to Rita Weeks of the Mickel Library at Converse College and Cecil Brown of the Spartanburg County Public Library for their assistance in securing numerous sources for me through interlibrary loans. I am also grateful to my friend Mike Corbin for helping to print several of the photographs that appear in this volume, and to my good wife, Katharine, for her steadfast encouragement.

PART ONE

Good Roads Progressivism

The Case for Good Roads

"I do not believe that there would have been a Civil War if we had had good roads, because the [North and South] would have been so mingled together," said Charles A. Bland, mayor of Charlotte, North Carolina. "I am satisfied," he continued, that "North Carolina was saved from the invasion of Sherman because the roads were so bad he could not get through."[1] Mayor Bland, one of the Tarheel State's most outspoken good roads advocates, was addressing a group of southerners assembled in Charlotte in 1902 to promote the idea of better roads. His strong words and reference to one of the South's great antiheroes were undoubtedly intended to arouse enthusiasm for the growing cause of good roads. Although automobiles were rarely seen in the South at that time, many southerners had become conscious of their miserable public roadways and wanted to do something to improve them. Progressive-minded southerners, therefore, included good roads on a long list of reforms, ranging from educational improvements to urban beautification, that, at the turn of the century, commanded their unwavering attention.

The issue of good roads, however, was not just a regional concern. It attracted the interest of a cross-section of thoughtful Americans and appealed, as well, to the reform impulses of other progressives who identified with the popular country life movement of the same era. Disciples of this persuasion, like those who subscribed to the tenets of good roads, attributed the burgeoning urban populations of the nation to deficiencies in rural life. They were convinced that the way to stem the tide of rural Americans leaving the farm for the city was to improve rural life, and one means to accomplish this was to upgrade the public roads. That way, they argued, farmers could take advantage of the cultural and economic opportunities cities offered without actually moving there; and likewise, urbanites could enjoy a respite from the rigidity and congestion of the city by being able to make brief jaunts to the country.

The group that did more than any other to foster good roads in the United States during the late nineteenth century was the League of American Wheelmen, an organization of bicyclists. One of their favorite pastimes was bicycle touring; but when confronted with roads that were not hard-surfaced, and muddy, rutted, and ill-maintained to match, bicycling was no pleasure. In order to pursue their recreation, Wheelmen, out of necessity, had to focus their attention on efforts to improve road conditions. They embarked on a full-fledged good roads campaign in 1888 and managed to influence Congress to pass legislation creating a national highway commission in 1892 and the Office of Road Inquiry within the Department of Agriculture in 1893. The majority of the league's membership, however, came from the urban-industrial Northeast, where there were more hard-surfaced roads and, generally, where Wheelmen could better afford the price of a bicycle. In 1897, only 2.3 percent of league members came from the South, and rarely did the organization sponsor tours that included any portion of the country below Pennsylvania.[2]

Deplorable roads were, indeed, one of the South's most visible deficiencies. Overland travel in the southern United States was difficult during most of the year but next to impossible during rainy winter months. Some communities in mountainous areas of the South were completely isolated from the outside world when rain and snow made the roads impassable, even for a mule. A day of rain could turn a rural road into a quagmire for a full week; and this affected not only local farmers who needed to transport their crops to market but hapless travelers who found themselves stranded in the middle of nowhere, stuck in the mud.

In his novel *The Reivers*, William Faulkner wrote about a stretch of road that his characters, Boon Hogganbeck, Ned the black coachman, and eleven-year-old Lucius Priest, encountered on their adventurous trip between northern Mississippi and Memphis, Tennessee. The year was 1905, and the road the three had been traveling in a vintage turn-of-the-century motorcar, "borrowed" from Lucius's grandfather, dipped down to cross the rain-swollen and appropriately named Hell Creek. "The road (the passage, whatever you would call it now,)" Lucius recalled,

> in front of us had not altered so much as it had transmogrified, exchanged mediums, elements. It now resembled a big receptacle of milk-infused coffee from which protruded here and there a few forlorn impotent hopeless odds and ends of sticks and brush and logs and an occasional hump of actual earth which looked startlingly like it had been deliberately thrown up by a plow.[3]

Unimproved roads were one of Faulkner's metaphors for a backward, undeveloped South. Bad roads and torturous traveling conditions were certainly very much a part of early twentieth-century southerners' way of life, and when a Georgian or North Carolinian told a bewildered, wayward traveler, "You can't get there from here!" chances were it was no joke.

By 1904, only a fraction over 4 percent, or 31,780, of the 790,284 miles of public roadways in the South were classified as "improved." And when one considers that most of this so-called improved road mileage was within urban rather than rural counties and consisted of stretches of roads that were macadamized or graded and covered with a thin layer of gravel or topsoil rather than hard-surfaced, it is not difficult to understand how backward the South really was. In several communities, like Mecklenburg and Buncombe counties in North Carolina, good roads enthusiasm had resulted in a few miles of these kinds of crude road improvements, but this was the exception and definitely not the rule.[4] To many thoughtful southerners at the turn of the century, therefore, it was painfully apparent that their roads were by far the worst in the entire nation and that little had been done to try to improve them.

In the South, the quest for good roads began as an effort to enhance rural life and stabilize the traditional values associated with farming, ideals that would later easily mesh with those of the country life movement. Efforts to improve the region's public roads commenced in the late nineteenth century as a part of Populism, a formidable campaign of farmers at the local, state, and national levels to bring about economic reforms beneficial to the agricultural classes. During the early twentieth century the good roads movement gained momentum as a regional progressive issue, and in the South, after its focus changed to a crusade to build interstate tourist highways, it enjoyed its greatest popularity. Finally, in the 1920s, once the federal government made a full financial commitment to improve public roadways nationwide, the movement subsided. During its years of inception, when many southerners perceived the improvement of the region's public roadways as a panacea for a variety of stubborn problems, good roads sentiment was given credit for generating a new spirit among rural southerners trapped by an economy and society that offered little hope of escape. Few reform causes in the South captured rural southerners' attention the way the good roads movement did.

Like the National Grange, whose local chapters were scattered primarily throughout the farming communities of the Midwest, by 1912 reform-oriented good roads organizations had spread across the South; and active, dues-paying members of county, state, and interstate good roads associations were as much a part of life in southern communities – both rural and urban, small and large – as Rotary and Lion's clubs' members are today. In the name of good roads, these local organizations produced a prodigious amount of literature, sponsored countless occasions for inspirational speeches, and held thousands of meetings which attracted the imagination of men and women interested in bettering their way of life. Typically, good roads campaigns in the South were convenient excuses for community gatherings and for expressions of people's faith in the future. They were also a ready-made cause for celebration and ballyhoo that spread throughout the South.[5]

Before the automobile age, the one group that stood to gain the most from good roads was farmers. Unimproved roads presented farmers in the South with many problems fundamental to their livelihood. Hauling crops to market over poor roads was expensive and very time-consuming. The United States Department of Agriculture estimated that poor roads cost American farmers approximately $600,000 in 1906. Part of that figure was the cost associated with farmers' working livestock. In Georgia in 1895 farmers paid $67,062 a day to feed their 268,248 horses and mules. Each day that wet weather made roads too muddy for these animals to work, farmers took a heavy loss. Furthermore, with good roads, one source argued, Georgia farmers could dispense with one-tenth of their draft animals and save $1,592,020.80 annually. Good roads promoters also advised farmers that greater savings could be realized when the stress and strain poor roads put on their valuable animals was taken into consideration. "I have seen a poor mule exert drawing a half-loaded wagon downhill during the muddy season," observed an Emory College professor and good roads advocate in 1896. He went on to cite statistics documenting that a horse could pull more than three times as much weight on a hard, smooth surface as over one made of gravel or dirt.[6]

Most southerners, like the Emory College professor, who fashioned themselves as progressive-minded, and who wrote or spoke about the benefits of good roads, focused primarily on farmers' problems. Among their arsenal of arguments was the claim that good roads prolonged animals' lives, which in the long run meant greater savings to the financially overburdened farmer. They also liked to point out that unimproved roads eliminated markets for many products. Being able to travel only within a relatively short radius of their farms due to poor roads, farmers were forced to market their produce when and where the weather permitted, which was not necessarily at times when prices were best. Good roads advocates repeatedly stressed that improved roads greatly increased farmland values and facilitated the substitution of more profitable crops for less profitable ones. But the main economic stimulus to improve farm conditions, reformers argued, was high railroad rates—over which farmers had absolutely no control. Poor roads were no alternative to the railroads when it came to getting valuable products quickly to market. But good roads were. And as railroad rates increased, so did the clamor to improve public thoroughfares.[7]

The cost of bad roads to farmers, however, was measured not solely in dollars and cents. In an era of rapid urbanization and industrialization, good roads were seen as a way of halting the decline in rural values and, at the same time, of providing farmers with a way of coping with the isolation and cultural backwardness inherent in their way of life. "The county dweller would be uplifted and stimulated" by better roads, claimed one authority on American agriculture, "and love of rural life would fill the nation." It was widely held that, because of impassable roads, thousands of young people in the South were unable to take advantage of social and cultural opportunities beyond the confines of their own fences. Good roads disciples were quick to conclude that, because of this isolation, young men and women living on farms were more likely to swap the boring drudgery of farm life for the glitter and excitement of the city. Had they been able to enjoy an occasional respite from life on the farm, the argument went, not as many would abandon farm life altogether and move to the city, causing urban populations to swell uncontrollably. "Money is not the only tribute nor the chief tribute that the country is making to the destructive demon of bad roads," said Dr. George T. Winston, president of the North Carolina State College of Agriculture and Mechanical Arts, in 1902.

> You will remember an ancient legend that the city of Thebes annually sent twelve of its choicest youths and maidens as a sacrifice to the island of Crete. Each year the vessel with white sails was manned in the harbor and the choicest boys and girls of the city were put in the vessel and carried as an offering to appease the wrath of the Minotaur. A similar sacrifice, far greater than millions in money, is made annually to our cities and towns by our citizens, the sacrifice of their choicest youth.[8]

Southerners attracted to the progressive benefits of good roads also prescribed improved roads as a cure for the South's educational woes, as a means of educational enlightenment, as a way of putting an end to the region's cultural provincialism, and even as a method of increasing church attendance. *The Southern Farm Gazette*, which circulated throughout Mississippi, Alabama, Louisiana,

Arkansas, and Tennessee, raised this question in 1909: "Of what use are schools and churches in country districts if for five to six months of the year country roads are so impassable that they cannot be attended?" It was also the opinion of a University of South Carolina education professor that any educational reforms were impossible to accomplish in the absence of good roads. "The best and quickest way to diffuse light in dark places," he wrote,

> is to bring the dark places within easy reach of the light. The better the highway between the two places, the nearer they are to each other. When good highways shall have been built, it will be found that a system of good schools is at least well on the way. Good roads and good schools are all but inseparable.[9]

If road improvements could bring educational reforms, they could also help liberate farm women isolated in rural, out-of-the-way parts of the South. Josephine Anderson Pearson, who grew up in rural Gallatin, Tennessee, and became a leader in women's education in the South during the early twentieth century, believed that good roads were more important to women than the right to vote. Pearson was a fierce opponent of women's suffrage. Between 1916 and 1920, she served as president of the Tennessee State Association Opposed to Woman's Suffrage, and in 1920 as president of the Southern Woman's League for the Rejection of the Susan B. Anthony Amendment, all the while appealing publicly and forcefully for good roads as a better and more discernible way to gain greater equality for women. "I seem to hear 'the whirr' of the automobile as it climbs the mountains and dashes along, recklessly determined of its mission to set us free," she stated in 1917,

> free from isolation and mud! We women are worse than slaves, considering everything, than the negroes were before the Civil War—slaves to the indifference of their men-folks as to whether we are shut up six months in the year and too busy to leave the other six months. . . . That long continued isolation . . . breeds insanity. . . . For every good day's work done by the men on [the roads] we will serve them the best dinner we can spread![10]

Good roads were indeed seen as a remedy for many of the drawbacks of rural life and as a way to restore some of the implicit rural American values thought lost in the wave of late nineteenth-century industrialization and urbanization. Thoughtful southerners like Pearson could not help but put road improvements at the top of their list of necessary progressive reform measures. "First and foremost construct a system of good roads," concluded a 1901 *Methodist Review* article. "This lies at the base of all rural life."[11] The litany of reasons why improved roads would be good for the South went on and on, limited only by the imagination of southern progressives. It would therefore seem that anyone who had even the slightest interest in agriculture or rural life would have enthusiastically jumped on the good roads bandwagon in the South. This, however, was not the case.

In 1806 Congress passed a law that established the first federally funded post road. It extended from Cumberland, Maryland, over the Appalachian Mountains, to St. Louis, Missouri. By 1838, when the last appropriation was made to pay for this road, the federal government had spent almost seven million dollars on the project. At about the same time Congress established this first post route, several members of Congress expressed a desire to have a direct overland mail connection between the nation's capital and the recently acquired port city of New Orleans. This led to some discussion about building a road that would run directly south from Washington and avoid the Appalachian mountain chain altogether. President Jefferson sent a surveyor to lay out this route, but before he completed the job, Congress decided to make use of an existing road over the same mountains to Knoxville, Tennessee, and from there to New Orleans. In the meantime, post road construction continued. By 1823, Congress had authorized the construction of almost a dozen post roads in the South, which, in addition to facilitating mail delivery, aided whites in their settlement of the region. In the period before the Civil War, however, post road construction was not a priority with Congress, and little money was allocated to pay for the opening of additional routes. Following the war, federal expenditures for road construction dried up altogether, and roads within the country—and especially those in the defeated South—went from bad to worse. Throughout the nineteenth century, therefore, at a time when European nations made great strides in road building, the United States put its financial resources primarily behind the construction of private railroads and, for the most part, ignored the development of any network of public highways to connect the individual states.

The reason was that, ever since the 1820s, southerners had adamantly opposed federal aid for internal improvements of any kind, and their strength in Congress during the first half of the century limited the amount of money spent on the construction of roads, as well as on canals and bridges. Southerners feared that increased federal spending would eventually lead to a higher tariff which would be detrimental to southern interests. But more importantly, advocates for the South, who called for a traditional reading of the Constitution when it came to the question of slavery, applied the same reasoning to the issue of internal improvements. Any effort on the part of Washington to appropriate money for internal improvements, they held, usurped the rights of the states and violated the Constitution.

As long as this was the accepted interpretation, there was little chance that public roads in the United States would receive the attention they needed. This drought of federal spending for road building finally came to an end in 1896 when Congress inaugurated Rural Free Delivery (RFD) and began building a series of post roads to facilitate mail delivery. There was no argument here, for the Constitution clearly authorized post road construction; and once RFD came to their communities, farmers were delighted at not having to pick up their mail at distant post offices. But RFD meant more than just convenience. Farmers quickly discovered the benefits improved post roads gave to the transportation of their crops to market. This realization, together with a policy adopted by the Post Office Department in 1899 prohibiting the construction of rural post routes where existing roads were altogether unfit for the successful delivery of the mail, brought forth an immediate response. Farmers were reported out in force repairing bridges, grading rutted surfaces, and smoothing otherwise impassable roads so that post road construction would not bypass their communities. For the first time, progressive farmers began organizing and joining local good roads associations. Two of the first in the South were the North Alabama Good Roads Association (founded in 1898) and the Good Roads Association of Asheville and Buncombe County, North Carolina (founded in 1899).[12]

After decades of stiff resistance to federally subsidized internal improvements, southerners began to see things differently. In 1902, three members of the Fifty-seventh United States Congress proposed good roads bills, and two of these members were from the South. Peter Johnston Otey of Virginia and John Stockdale Rhea of Kentucky introduced legislation that would have authorized the federal government to fund the construction of public roads in the existing forty-five states and four territories – quite a departure from the South's traditional opposition to such measures. This legislation was undoubtedly the result of pressure from good roads and farm groups which had become active in lobbying for road reforms. Congressman Rhea had particularly close ties to farmers, having been first elected to the House in 1897 as a member of the Populist Party. Nevertheless, these bills and many subsequent ones concerning road improvements died before reaching the House floor for debate; and almost a decade and a half passed before Congress provided enough money to begin to help southerners rid themselves of the tremendous problems unimproved roads caused.[13]

In the meantime, the business of building and improving roads in the United States was carried out at local governmental levels. But it was here that the majority of farmers balked. Ever since colonial times, southerners had paid their local taxes by spending a day or so each year actually working – with whatever farm equipment was available – on the improvement of their communities' public roads. This practice spanned two centuries, and as late as 1912, every southern state used the method. In fact, each of the eleven former Confederate states had a law that required its male citizens to do road work every year. "All male persons over eighteen and under fifty," read the Mississippi statute, "unless exempt by law, shall be required annually to perform not to exceed ten days of work on the public roads." The penalty for not working was usually a nominal fine, and in some cases, notably Tennessee, residents could send substitutes.

What this system meant to financially strapped farmers was that they had to pay no out-of-pocket taxes to finance road maintenance and construction in their communities. After all, farmers argued, why place an additional financial burden on an already depressed segment of the economy when road improvements could be accomplished the same way they always had? Progressive farm groups in the South, like the National Farmers' Union, took the position that, since improved public roads would be of such great benefit to them, farmers should be willing to be taxed to have better access to marketplaces. But for the most part, farmers remained relatively content with things as they were. The roads got some of the attention they needed, which pleased local officials, and farmers paid no taxes. For this reason the issue of good roads may have ranked as high with farmers in the South as other reform issues like a graduated income tax, rural credits, railroad regulation, or parcel post, but it rarely got beyond the rhetorical stage. In showing support for RFD, many farmers simply believed they were also endorsing the idea of good roads that essentially required the federal government, and not farmers, to underwrite the cost of road construction.[14]

Before 1916 the statute labor system was the most widely used method of building and maintaining roads in the South. But it was carried out at the county rather than the state level, which made fraud and noncompliance commonplace. Most citizens never spent a day doing road work, preferring either to pay the small annual fine or to enlist the assistance of a local politician who had the power to grant a permanent exemption from the requirement. Those who, on the other hand, complied with the law and performed road work each year, commonly observed the few days away from their normal chores as a holiday. An article published in *Scribner's Magazine* in 1889 provided the following account of a typical day working on the roads:

> Arriving on the ground long after the usual time of beginning work, the road-makers proceeded to discuss the general question of road-making and other matters of public concern, until slow-acting conscience convinces them that

they should be about their task. They then with much deliberation take the mud out of the road-side ditches, if, indeed, the way is ditched at all, and plaster the same on the center of the road. A plough is brought into requisition, which destroys the best part of the road, that which is partly grassed and bushgrown, and the soft mass is heaped up to the central parts of the way. . . . An hour or two is consumed at noon-day lunch and further discussion of public and private matters. A little work is done in the afternoon, and at the end of the day the road making is abandoned until next year.[15]

The other means of road building in the South during the late nineteenth and early twentieth centuries was convict labor. By 1910, every southern state legislature had authorized local governments, both county and municipal, to make use of convicts incarcerated within their jurisdictions in the building and maintenance of public thoroughfares. Each southern state made use of its convicts in a different way. In Louisiana, for example, by the fall of 1909, Governor Jared Y. Sanders had persuaded prison officials to establish a network of labor camps throughout the state, each consisting of twenty-four convicts. It was Sanders's idea that road work should be their main concern. Using convict labor between 1904 and 1909, the state of Georgia managed to more than double its improved road mileage; and it was the opinion of the director of the Office of Public Roads, Logan Waller Page, that "if all the state and county prisoners in the South were placed upon the roads . . . a wonderful reformation could be brought about with a comparatively small cash outlay."[16]

Undeniably, convict labor was responsible for much of the road improvement work done in the South before 1910. But like statute labor, the convict labor system was always ripe for abuse. It was not at all uncommon to find convicts working on private property rather than in the public domain; and because of the so-called "convict lease" system, which was practiced widely throughout the South, public roads received little attention. Convict brokers leased convicts from local prisons and then found owners of mines, brickyards, and turpentine distilleries who paid them for the laborers' time. It was easy, however, for public officials to exert their influence, bypass the broker and, for the price of a small bribe paid to a prison official, obtain convicts' services free of charge. Thus small groups of influential citizens in the South profited greatly from convict labor; but rarely did public projects, like road building, get the attention they deserved. "Convict lease" became such a problem in Georgia that in 1908, after the Atlanta *Georgian* started a public campaign against the practice, Governor Hoke Smith, a reformer, called the state legislature into special session to outlaw the long established and much abused system for good.[17]

Considering the number of southerners who were required by law to perform road work each year, and the number of convicts also available, very little was actually accomplished. This affirms how widely abused were the most relied-upon means for road construction in the South. But to make matters worse, the meager effort that was put forth often proved detrimental to the roads that were in such desperate need of repair. Farmers knew a lot more about growing corn and cotton than improving roads, and it was a commonly held belief that working on the public roads required absolutely no training or experience. As a result, not only did the quality of public roads vary from county to county, but in many cases, the roads would have been better off left alone entirely. Long after the campaign for good roads had begun in the South, however, most communities still relied upon statute and convict labor as the principal means of building new roads and maintaining existing ones.

In 1912, southerners invented another means to improve their roads. "Good Roads Days" first began to be practiced in Alabama, and by 1913 Kansas, Missouri, and North Carolina adopted similar observances. The Tarheel State received a great deal of publicity regarding its efforts and consequently gained the reputation as one of the most progressive good roads states in the South. In September 1913, North Carolina Governor Locke Craig announced that, for the first time, two days of the following November would be observed statewide as Good Roads Days. He called upon "all patriotic people throughout the state to work upon the public roads and refrain from all other occupations" on the two appointed days. "Let no man be above this work," Craig preached, "nor forget his duty to himself and his neighbors." Progress was made in many of North Carolina's one hundred counties, the most being accomplished in Buncombe County (Asheville), where Craig himself rolled up his sleeves and donned a pair of overalls to wield a pick and shovel. On the average, a few hundred people in each of the participating counties, armed with all sorts of equipment, heeded the governor's plea. Their efforts, however, far outweighed the pitifully few miles of new roads built or the short stretches of existing roads improved. In Anson County, for example, 259 men managed to build only one-half mile of road in the two-day period, and similarly sparse accomplishments were common throughout the state.[18]

It was clear to many progressive-minded southerners interested in good roads that, if communities had to rely upon local resources in the form of statute and convict labor and an occasional Good Roads Day, there was little hope of even beginning to eliminate the region's miserable roads and the problems they caused. By 1910, there were signs of improvement but not enough to make any substantial difference. Twenty out of Texas's twenty-four counties had approved bond issues to fund road improvements, and according to the Birmingham *Age-Herald*, with the exception of Kentucky, Arkansas, and South Carolina, every southern state was doing the same. This undeniably progressive achievement, however, came twenty-one years after New Jersey became the first state in the nation to adopt a general county road law permitting counties to issue bonds for the construction of broken-stone roads. Still, counties in the South wishing to upgrade their roads by special taxation or bonded indebtedness had to organize local referenda, and it was because of this cumbersome process that road improvement measures failed more often than they passed. In Moore County, North Carolina, for example, good roads supporters succeeded in getting a road improvement proposal before the voters in 1907. But when the votes were counted, the conservative tendencies of Moore County farmers prevailed. Good roads were voted down by a wide margin of between five hundred and six hundred votes. "The road over which I travel is good enough for me," was the consensus opinion voiced by one farmer. "Why should I vote to tax myself to help others?"[19]

Unable to make much headway in getting their communities' roads improved, or in influencing state legislators to fund road improvements, early leaders of the good roads movement in the South turned their attention to education as a means of dispelling the myth that road construction was as easy as plowing, and as a way to convince public officials that miracles could not be accomplished in the absence of money. As early as 1894, the technical aspects of road building were being discussed in North Carolina. In the summer of that year, the University of North Carolina and the North Carolina Road Improvement Association – an early populist-oriented good roads organization – held a conference in Chapel Hill addressing proper road building procedures. Formal training in road construction, however, was slow to come to the South. In North Carolina, Joseph Hyde Pratt, working from 1906 to 1917 as the state geologist, provided technical assistance in the proper methods of road building. Pratt's work received wide attention and encouraged southerners in other states interested in road improvements to seek professional assistance. But road improvement training still remained the exception rather than the rule. As late as 1917, some state governments – mostly those in the Northeast – required that road improvements be made with skilled supervision. Only three southern states, Alabama, North Carolina, and Texas, had progressed that far.

Part of the problem was that in the South professional training in road improvements and highway construction was unheard of. The Massachusetts Institute of Technology had endowed its first chair in civil engineering and had provided funds for the study of road systems abroad in 1890. Twenty-three years later, in 1913 courses in the science of road building began to be offered in southern colleges and universities. Ten institutions of higher education in the South began to train civil engineering students in proper highway construction techniques. The Department of Engineering at the University of South Carolina held a series of lectures and recitals covering the basic principles of road locations as well as the construction and maintenance of earth, gravel, sand-clay, and macadam roads. Another southern university that began road maintenance courses in 1913 was the Alabama Polytechnique Institute at Auburn (now Auburn University): a year later, the University of the South at Sewanee, Tennessee, offered its first course in highway construction. Good roads advocates must have been particularly convincing in Kentucky, where each county awarded two scholarships annually to students at the University of Kentucky who showed interest in highway engineering.[20]

Assisting good roads organizations in gaining acceptance for these new courses was the Office of Public Roads Inquiry, whose principal functions, from its inception in 1893, were education and investigation. This bureau of the United States Department of Agriculture disseminated information regarding approved road building techniques through two sources: its publications and a practice begun in 1896 in which trained engineers, using state-of-the-art machinery rather than farming equipment, actually demonstrated how to construct a road. The short stretches of roadway built in many communities throughout the country as a result of this practice were known as "object lesson" roads, and they were generally paid for by the communities in which they were built.

"Object lesson" roads served three purposes. First, they introduced local road builders to the correct methods of construction. Second, they demonstrated the advantages of properly built roads, with the idea of stimulating public sentiment for road improvements and arousing greater good roads support. And finally, "object lesson" roads revealed the appealing fact that local materials could be successfully used to defray construction costs.[21]

"Object lesson" roads were first built in the South during the winter of 1901-2 as part of a tour organized by the National Good Roads Association, the Office of Public Roads Inquiry, and the Southern Railroad Company. Samuel Spencer, president of the Southern Railroad, promoted the idea of a Good Roads Train that would tour the Deep South. During the spring and summer of 1901, a Good Roads Train ran on the Illinois Central Line through the southern states of Louisiana, Mississippi, Tennessee, and Kentucky, but what Spencer envisioned was much more ambitious. He showed an interest in road improvements because he understood roads to be an extension of railway lines and realized that road improvements in the South could greatly benefit his business. Being a fixed system of transportation, railroads served only the most populated and profitable markets and consequently needed to be supplemented by rural road networks. Without well-maintained roads over which products and raw materials could be transported from farms to centralized railheads and then moved by train from the South to other regions of the United States, the Southern Railroad could never expect to earn the kind of profits that Spencer had in mind.

The Southern Railroad Good Roads Train left Alexandria, Virginia, on the afternoon of 29 October 1901. The black steam-engine, with the name "Southern Railroad Company" clearly stenciled on the side, pulled a camp car of laborers, ten to twelve cars loaded with the road building machinery of seven leading manufacturers, and two cars that housed the train's official delegation. This included Martin Dodge, director of the Office of Public Roads Inquiry; W. H. Moore and R. W. Richardson, both officials of the National Good Roads Association; and a dozen or so manufacturers' representatives.

Before it chugged into Charlottesville, Virginia, on 2 April 1902 for its final of eighteen stops the train toured six southern states, covered 4,037 miles, and at each stop engineers supervised the construction of a short stretch of "object lesson" roadway. Each stop lasted several days and was occasion for much speech making and ceremony about the worth of good roads. "Nothing more deeply concerns the general welfare of our people than this movement," said South Carolina Governor Miles B. McSweeny when the train was in Columbia. "South Carolina . . . is but just awakening to the value of good roads." In Raleigh, North Carolina, on 12 February 1902, Governor Charles B. Aycock lamented that "the question of good roads touches us at every point. The roads are the only thing in this State of which I am ashamed, because they are in a condition that is without excuse." At its last stop, in Charlottesville, Samuel Spencer offered a brief summary of what he concluded to be a successful venture. "It has attracted some attention . . . for an improvement which I regard as the most important one now before us in the development of the South."

The close association of Spencer with the Good Roads Train, as well as his advocacy of improved roads for the South, must have been more than a little confusing to farmers. Here was a man who espoused all the good roads rhetoric about saving farmers money in hauling costs and yet who, on the other hand, symbolized the very thing farmers had been struggling against for years: high freight rates. This, however, did not seem to inhibit attendance at Good Roads Train functions. Because the train stopped only in urban areas, governors and state legislators sought to notify as many people as possible beyond the reach of the cities so that they could plan to be in town when the train was there. Word went out to publishers, editors, county commissioners, county road supervisors, local law enforcement officials, administrators of educational institutions, and members of the very few good roads organizations existing at that early date. At several stops conventions were held, and governors, members of Congress, state legislators, and university presidents stood before crowds of onlookers to preach the gospel of good roads. The excitement the train generated did much to encourage a progressive spirit of road building. In Winston-Salem, North Carolina, on 30 October 1901 – one day after the Good Roads Train departed Alexandria – approximately four hundred good roads enthusiasts gathered and formed the first of fourteen good roads associations spawned by the train's presence.[22] (See table.)

The Office of Public Roads Inquiry hailed the formation of these organizations as one of the "more noteworthy industrial achievements [to have] taken place in the United States in recent years," and one it hoped would have a significant impact "on the development of one of the great sections of the country." Throughout the next decade, reformers who saw road improvements as a means of augmenting rural values and stabilizing life on the farm sought to extend their influence through these organizations. Seeking as

Good Roads Associations Formed in the South, 1901-2

Date Formed	Location	Organization
30 October 1901	Winston-Salem, N.C.	Northwestern Good Roads Association of North Carolina
4 November 1901	Asheville, N.C.	Appalachian Good Roads Association
8-9 November 1901	Greenville, Tenn.	East Tennessee Good Roads Association
13-15 November 1901	Chattanooga, Tenn.	Chattanooga District Good Roads Association
26-30 November 1901	Mobile, Ala.	South Alabama Good Roads Association
2 December 1901	Montgomery, Ala.	Alabama State Good Roads Association
9 December 1901	Atlanta, Ga.	Georgia State Good Roads Association
16 December 1901	Greenville, S.C.	South Carolina Good Roads Association
13-18 January 1902	Columbus, Ga.	Chattahoochee Valley Good Roads Association
20 January 1902	Augusta, Ga.	Savannah Valley Good Roads Association
10 February 1902	Raleigh, N.C.	North Carolina Good Roads Association
3 March 1902	Lynchburg, Va.	Midland–James River Valley Good Roads Association
13 March 1902	Danville, Va.	Interstate Good Roads Association
17 March 1902	Richmond Va.	Virginia State Good Roads Association

much interest in good roads at the local level as possible, leaders
of the associations formed during the winter of 1901–2 encouraged
the growth of more grass-roots organizations. Shortly after the North
Carolina Good Roads Association was born in Raleigh in 1902,
for example, founding members tried to appoint at least one vice-
president from each county. By 1912, hundreds of good roads clubs
and associations had cropped up throughout the South. In its *Official
Good Roads Yearbook for 1912,* the American Highway Association
(AHA) listed affiliation with 20 good roads organizations in Alabama, 3 in Arkansas, 25 in Florida, 53 in Georgia, 3 in Kentucky,
5 in Louisiana, 4 in Mississippi, 65 in North Carolina, 26 in South
Carolina, 13 in Tennessee, 30 in Texas, and 27 in Virginia. This
made 274, or 60 percent of all the good roads organizations in the
United States considered by the AHA as its affiliates.[23] Some of
these organizations, of course, were more active than others. But
generally they held regular meetings, adopted resolutions, sponsored long-distance automobile endurance contests, assisted county
and municipal governments in road building, sought clarification
in court for road funding measures, and lobbied state and local
politicians to appropriate road improvement revenue.

During this time, when the good roads movement in the South
was gaining momentum, no single individual emerged as its leader.
Those who spoke in favor of good roads defied any particular
categorizing. University presidents, college professors, newspaper
editors, publishers, judges, ministers, attorneys, engineers, farmers,
doctors, and southerners in all walks of life were among the throng
who conceived of road improvements as an answer to the region's
backwardness. Many southern politicians gravitated to the movement. Good roads were as safe a political topic as any aspiring
office seeker or veteran politician might find. It neither raised
eyebrows nor created controversy. Financing was rarely mentioned;
only the promise of a better South was heard. Many southern politicians preached the doctrine of good roads to voters, but by 1910
only two had gained notoriety: Asbury C. Latimer of South Carolina and John H. Bankhead, Sr., of Alabama.

Latimer was the son of an Abbeville County, South Carolina, farmer who died and left young Latimer, still in his teens, with a debt-ridden, five-hundred-acre farm. After three years he managed to clear the debt and, in 1880, moved to Anderson County in the Upstate. His early experience with indebtedness taught him the harsh lessons of farming, and after living in Anderson County for a few years, Latimer emerged as one of the organizers and leading proponents of the South Carolina Farmers Alliance. In 1894 he represented South Carolina farmers at the Alliance convention in Ocala, Florida, and supported the long list of agricultural demands ratified at that meeting. His political career began in 1890 when he refused the Democratic Party's nomination for lieutenant governor on the ticket with Benjamin R. Tillman. Chairing the Democratic Party of Anderson County between 1890 and 1892, Latimer instead made a name for himself by endorsing equal rights and farm reform measures. In 1892 Upstate South Carolinians elected him to represent the Third Congressional District, a seat he held until 1903, when the state legislature chose him to serve in the United States Senate.

In the House, Latimer showed his Populist colors by supporting legislation like the Rural Free Delivery bill and a legislative measure intended to establish a more equitable system for seed distribution. In 1896 he spoke in favor of a measure long supported by the Populist Party that would have authorized the federal government to issue silver certificates to meet temporary revenue shortages. After citing statistics that he believed showed how deeply in debt the government actually was, he chided his congressional colleagues:

> How any man who has been elected to a position in this honorable body can keep from feeling like a traitor to his country when he votes to strike down silver and meet these obligations with blood-sought, blood-bought, sweat-bought, and conscience-bought gold is more than I can understand.

Latimer was a passionate populist, but it was not until he reached the Senate that he began to speak out for good roads. On 14 January 1904 he made his first speech in the Senate on behalf of a resolution he introduced directing the secretary of agriculture to furnish the Senate with cost estimates for a national road improvement cam-

(*Left*): Asbury Churchill Latimer (1851–1908) served in the U.S. House of Representatives from the Third Congressional District of South Carolina from 1892 until 1903 and as one of the Palmetto State's two U.S. senators from 1903 until his death in 1908. As a populist, Latimer strongly advocated the use of federal funds to improve and maintain rural farm-to-market roads. Courtesy of the Library of Congress.
(*Right*): John Hollis Bankhead, Sr. (1842–1920), United States senator from Alabama from 1908 until 1920, was instrumental in getting the Federal Highway Act of 1916 passed. He was the last Confederate Army veteran to serve in Congress. Courtesy of the Alabama Department of Archives and History.

paign. He later introduced a bill that called for the appropriation of twenty-four million dollars and the establishment of a framework for a cooperative effort between the federal government and the individual states in the construction of new and the improvement of existing public roads in the United States. By requiring the states to furnish the necessary rights-of-way and to maintain the new roadways once they had been constructed, Latimer believed that he had cleverly sidestepped the traditional constitutional objections to federal involvement in road building. "None of the powers of the states are interfered with," he said, "the bill simply deals with the right of the Federal Government to appropriate money to aid in constructing public roads for the good of all the people."

According to the South Carolina senator, since farmers were "the producers of the food products and many of the raw materials upon which the world lives and grows fat in body and finance," it was the moral duty of Congress to shift the burden of paying for road improvements off the backs of farmers and adopt a more equitable system for raising road revenues. He proposed to accomplish this by requiring the states to levy an excise tax not only on tangible property like land, domestic animals, household furniture, and farm implements but on stocks, bonds, shares in corporations, and other securities. Without taxing this second category of wealth, Latimer argued, "the tax would fall most heavily upon the very class [farmers] who already bear the cost of building and maintaining the roads."[24]

Over the next four years, between 1904 and 1908, Latimer worked unsuccessfully to get his bill passed, all the while enthusiastically introducing and supporting legislative appropriations to maintain and upgrade the tiny Office of Public Roads Inquiry within the Department of Agriculture. When Latimer died on 20 February 1908, while still in office, the campaign for road improvements was gaining strength, and within the United States Senate, Latimer's role as chief spokesman for good roads was quickly filled. John H. Bankhead, Sr., a first-year senator from Alabama, picked up where Latimer left off.

Bankhead neither espoused the rhetoric nor entertained the same strong grass-roots convictions as his deceased colleague from South Carolina. Nevertheless, the Alabamian's roots were as rural as Latimer's. He was born on a back-country antebellum farm near Moscow (now Lamar County), Alabama, and before serving in the Confederate Army, worked as a farmer. Between 1865 and 1866, he served in the lower house of the Alabama legislature and, after Reconstruction, one term in the state senate. Governor Rufus W. Cobb appointed Bankhead warden of the state prison system in 1881, and while he held that position, he instituted a number of reforms. Five years later, in 1886 Bankhead once again ran for public office and was successful in capturing the Sixth United States Congressional seat from Alabama. He held this office for ten consecutive terms, until 1906, when Spanish-American War hero Richard Pearson Hobson managed to unseat him. While in the House, Bankhead was a member of the Committee on Public Buildings and Grounds. As its chairman, he oversaw construction projects all over the nation, including the Library of Congress in Washington and dozens of public buildings in his home state. In 1898, he became a member of the Committee on Rivers and Harbors and began a more earnest effort to use his position to address the concerns of his rural constituents.

Bankhead was of the opinion that, in the absence of competition, railroads could charge whatever freight rates they wanted. Adopting legislation to regulate railroads, he felt, was not necessarily the best nor the only means to ensure fairness. He foresaw the construction of a well-developed waterway system throughout the farming states as a means of providing the competition railroads needed to lower freight rates. The congressional appropriation of funds to canalize the Warrior River near Tuscaloosa, Alabama, and to dredge Mobile Bay Harbor were the direct results of Bankhead's influence on the Rivers and Harbors Committee and clear evidence of his desire to challenge the railroad monopoly.

These very visible projects earned Bankhead a statewide reputation, and in 1907, after being out of Congress for the first time in twenty years, he won the nomination of the Democratic Party of Alabama to assume the first United States Senate seat to become available. His campaign platform was an extension of his work to develop navigable rivers and harbors; only this time it focused on the improvement of public roads. Less than a year later, Senator John Tyler Morgan died, and after approval from the state legislature, Alabama Governor Braxton Bragg Comer appointed Bankhead to finish Morgan's unexpired term.

When Bankhead took his seat in the Sixtieth Congress, Populist issues remained very much a part of southern politics, and politicians like himself were beginning to view federal legislation as more of an aid than a burden to their constituencies. In 1906, while still a member of the House, Bankhead introduced a resolution calling for the federal government to begin to fund road building, and that, together with his good roads senatorial campaign, identified him as a high-ranking public official interested in road reform measures. At home in Alabama, Bankhead had long been an advocate of road improvements. He had helped organize the North Alabama Good Roads Association, one of the first such organizations in the South, served as one of its vice-presidents for almost ten years before beginning his senatorial career, and had long listened to the complaints of farmers about needed road improvements.[25]

Bankhead was sworn in as a United States senator in January 1908, and it was not long before he made his first speech on the subject of good roads. He began by saying that, while Congress had done much to aid railroad and maritime transportation in the United States, it had neglected the public roads over which, he claimed, 90 percent of the nation's internal commerce moved. He cited statistics to show how badly farmers suffered from poor roads and complained that Congress had been unfair to "that great, silent, patient element of our population, the American farmer." Then he answered critics who argued that federal aid to road improvement amounted to socialism, something Bankhead called paternalism. "If they are asking the Federal Government to prescribe our daily bread," he said,

> or . . . to clothe our bodies, that would be paternalism pure and simple. Such a function of the Government would be enervating; it would destroy individuality and repress all energy and ambition. We only ask that it contribute a portion of the cost of improving our public roads, and, in making this contribution, it will . . . open up new and improved channels to marts of trade and commerce, stimulate industrial enterprise, inspire every citizen of the rural districts with a brighter hope and a higher ambition, and add a new tie to bind him with increased loyalty and patriotism to his country.

He also admonished Congress for spending such large sums of money on the internal improvements of other countries, notably Cuba, Puerto Rico, and the Philippines, while doing nothing for Americans at home. "They claim these roads [in other countries] are for civilization," he said. "Well, we need a little civilization ourselves."[26]

Bankhead's eloquence in articulating the plight of farmers aroused the interest of at least two national political figures. In speeches before the National Good Roads Congress Convention in Chicago during the summer of 1908, both William Jennings Bryan and President Theodore Roosevelt spoke of the great benefits improved roads would mean to American farmers. That same summer, both the Democratic and Republican parties gave approval to plans under which the federal government would aid in the construction and maintenance of public roads in the United States. But still it amounted only to talk. In early 1910, Bankhead introduced several good roads measures in the Senate, one of which passed. Although it authorized Congress to appropriate road improvement funds, the new law had little effect since state and local governments had to match each federal dollar with two of their own. Even though Bankhead was optimistic about Washington's involvement in the funding of a national road improvement campaign – and between December 1911 and July 1912 some sixty good roads bills were introduced in Congress – clearly at this point most members of Congress were not.[27]

By 1910, from the lowest to the highest level of government in the United States, little had been done to help southerners rid themselves of a system of roads that the federal government openly admitted was the poorest in the entire country and needed attention "more urgently than in the North." Neither the federal government nor any state legislature in the South, with the exceptions of Alabama and Virginia, provided any direct financial assistance to local governments for road improvements. Many southerners intent on the notion that road improvements were one salvation for the region's backwardness had worked hard to have better roads, and their goals for the future South meshed nicely with those of other progressive reform campaigns underway at the same time. Antiquated laws and a rural population which in theory approved of road reform measures but in practice was unwilling to underwrite, however, hampered their efforts.

While a part of a larger and more widespread effort to improve farm life, good roads progressivism in the South during the first decade of the twentieth century evidenced strong ties to late nine-teenth-century American Populism. Nevertheless, the effort to get the South out of the mud and onto smooth- or hard-surfaced roads sputtered along for ten or so years, failing to attract the serious support of enough southerners to make Congress sit up and take notice. Less than 7 percent of the South's public roads by 1910 were classified as improved. In the six years between 1904 and 1910 – a time when other states outside the South made significant progress toward better road transportation – southern states managed to increase their unimproved road mileage by not even 3 percent. In 1911, 24 percent of the public roads in Connecticut were im-proved; in Indiana almost 37 percent were no longer impassable during the winter months; and in Massachusetts, almost half were listed as improved.[28]

If the good roads movement in the South had accomplished anything by 1910, it had succeeded in publicizing the need of farmers for better roadways. But all of the progressive rhetoric, organiza-tional effort, and promotional schemes in the name of good roads had not aroused enough people to make a difference between hav-ing improved roads and suffering along year after year with the miserable conditions of the past. No strong organization emerged to lead the good roads movement or hold southerners' interest long enough and steadfastly enough to realize any significant gain. And because farmers adamantly refused to pay additional taxes to have better roads, neither the Farmers' Union nor the Farmers' Alliance listed good roads at the top of their lists of reform priorities. Pro-gressive arguments about the economic rewards farmers would reap from good roads, as well as the social and economic opportunities improved roads would bring, were not realistic or convincing enough to capture the imagination of a broad segment of the South's popula-tion, either.

Many southerners perceived the issue of good roads as concern-ing only farmers. After all, up to that time, this had been the main emphasis. Furthermore, had not farmers complained for years about their problems and proposed reform measures considered even more far-reaching and radical than the construction of a system of all-weather farm-to-market roads? Railroads and other businesses directly related to agriculture clearly benefited from well-maintained roads; but to the vast majority of southerners who listened to the rhetoric and in some way identified with the concept of a "New South," the good roads message was too vague. To this group – more steeped in the fine art of boosterism than their country cousins – the most important question of how improved roads would benefit businesses, enhance profits, and more quickly bring about the dream of an urban-industrial South remained unanswered.

Beginning in 1908, about the same time intrepid northern motorists in small numbers started to trickle south in their supply-laden automobiles, southern business leaders, real estate developers, and New South prophets gradually began to become more involved in the quest for better roads. Over the next decade the good roads movement in the South evolved into an effort to improve long-distance tourist highways and slipped out of the controlling grasp of those who had different expectations of what improved local networks of roads could accomplish for the impoverished region. Highways, as we shall see in Part Two, helped culturally unify the South with the rest of the nation, but they had nothing to do with the realization of the original objectives of good roads progressivism. As the nature and thrust of the good roads movement changed and "highway progressives" bludgeoned the public with the message that highway construction was the way to achieve the long-sought-after dream of a "New South," the modern, slick, comfortable, public-relations-oriented South began to come of age.

The Promise of Accessibility

Between 1910 and 1920 automobiling in America ceased to be a recreational pursuit enjoyed primarily by the wealthy and became a pastime of the middle class. Cheaper cars put the cost of ownership within reach of people of modest means; touring became a favorite recreation; and this unprecedented use of motor vehicles did more to stimulate interest in road improvements nationwide than all the good roads rhetoric and political arm-twisting of the previous two decades.

Like their bicycle predecessors, automobile owners quickly discovered that poorly maintained roads drastically inhibited their mobility. Rutted, muddy roads caused Sunday afternoon excursions to be anything but delightful and, for all but an eccentric few, made the thought of a cross-country tour in a motorcar out of the question. Their twentieth-century automobiles, the very symbols of modernity, were of pitifully little use on nineteenth-century horse-and-buggy trails. Rather than support existing good roads organizations, however, many automobilists joined automobile clubs, like the American Automobile Association, that championed motorists' causes with extraordinary enthusiasm and went to great lengths to publicize the need to improve public roadways in the United States. Automobile owners as well as automobile manufacturers, who viewed the nation's unimproved thoroughfares as a major obstacle to the successful sale of motor vehicles, wanted highways for touring purposes, and not necessarily to reduce farmers' hauling costs, enhance rural land values, or any of the other reasons constantly cited by reformers. Through slick monthly publications, like the *American Motorist, Travel, Automobile, Motor World,* and others, this interest group got its message of improved roads across to the newly mobile American middle class. This accomplishment helped provide an entirely new direction for the good roads movement, and within a few short years, the effects were being felt in the South.

Progressive reform efforts in the South, like the good roads movement, as we have seen, attracted the support of not only farmers but thoughtful, educated professionals. At the same time that these doctors, lawyers, and educators proposed reforms to improve their region, they embraced a definition of progress that was not quite as familiar to their farming neighbors. This brand of progressivism gave great emphasis to economic development as the means by which the goal of an urban-industrial South would be achieved. Middle-class southerners who championed this notion of progress were able to combine the convictions of reformers and the instincts of capitalists with little difficulty, and after the emphasis of the good roads movement shifted to the construction of interstate tourist highways instead of local farm-to-market roads, no other manifestation of southern progressivism evidenced this contradiction more clearly.

Once automobile tourism presented unprecedented opportunities for making money, it was not at all difficult for many southerners—some who were already involved as well as others who had taken little previous interest in good roads efforts—to envision the prospect of road improvements as a means of generating a new economic vitality for the South. These people were for the most part young, upwardly mobile, and decidedly middle-class. Many regarded themselves as forward-looking, progressive-minded men and women and listened intently as business leaders, who also had paid little previous attention to the benefits of road improvements, redefined the goals of good roads progressivism in the South.

When this new enthusiasm for good roads blossomed, the dream of uniting the North and South over improved interstate highways became a popular theme often heard when good roads were the topic of discussion. This was not a philosophical proximity that southerners were after, but one in which the South might finally share in the industrial wealth of the North. Atlanta Mayor Robert F. Maddox expressed this mood of optimism in a speech he made in 1909 to a group of northern industrialists gathered in the Georgia capital to celebrate the opening of the first national automobile show ever held in the South. "The automobile," he said,

> will weld together . . . the most distant parts of our beloved country. Georgia stands here today and, extending one hand to far-off Massachusetts in the east and the other to distant Wisconsin in the west, gives hospitable greeting to all, and promises that she will take her place with her sisters in every section . . . to push our reunited land to greater prosperity and greater glory.[1]

By 1915 the legions of good roads apostles in the South were swollen with chamber of commerce members, bank presidents, sales representatives, real estate agents, and trade board members. This group was on the rise in the South, and with its ongoing campaign for a "New South," already had the public's attention. It was, therefore, not difficult to shift the balance of good roads progressivism away from farm-oriented issues and to focus on how the South might better itself financially by improving the public thoroughfares that led outsiders into the region. As the new agents for good roads, these self-styled highway progressives paid only lip service to rural development issues and mentioned the concerns of farmers only as a means of getting them on the bandwagon to construct tourist highways. To highway progressives, good roads in the South clearly meant increased tourism, and that translated into economic well-being.

As an overwhelming wave of New South hyperbole promoting interstate tourist highways began to command more and more public attention, the early grass-roots organizations that southerners had formed to work for the construction of farm-to-market roads became lost. The good roads movement in the South became primarily a highway movement; regional good roads publications, like *Dixie Highway*, *Southern Good Roads*, and *Dixie Borderland Highways Magazine*, combining and refining the new-found goals of good roads and tourism, emerged; and a new leadership forged entirely new good roads organizations – highway associations – to carry out the objective of attracting automobile tourists. The first of these organizations began with the help of a transplanted Massachusetts real estate developer who found himself stuck with 5,890 acres of partially developed land in the remote Sandhills section of North Carolina without good reason to develop it further or any feasible way of selling it.

Leonard Tufts was not at all like his father, James Walker Tufts, who bought the North Carolina acreage in 1895 for a dollar an acre with the intention of constructing a health resort. The elder Tufts had made a fortune in the soda fountain business, and toward the end of his life, like other nineteenth-century millionaires, turned his attention away from business and toward philanthropy. In 1890 he built several tenement houses for immigrant workers in Charlestown, Massachusetts, and a year later established a mutual benefit association in his own Boston factory which paid employees both disability and death benefits. Tufts also found the humanitarian efforts of New England Unitarian Minister Edward Everett Hale particularly to his liking and cooperated with Hale's popular "Lend a Hand" work among tuberculosis victims in Boston's North End.

At that time tuberculosis was thought to be a congenital disease, and with Hale's encouragement, Tufts went looking for a place with a healthful climate where tuberculosis patients and their families could go for convalescent care. His purchase of the North Carolina acreage near Southern Pines, already an established resort for tuberculosis invalids, was made with this idea in mind. Tufts first called his development "Pinalia" and later "Pinehurst." And within a few months of its purchase, he hired renowned landscape architect Frederick Law Olmsted, who was at work near Asheville, North Carolina, on George Washington Vanderbilt's colossal Biltmore Estate, to draw up the general plan for "a village with open park spaces and winding streets that retain their usefulness by following lines of beauty." Although Olmsted never visited Pinehurst, Tufts paid the firm of Olmsted, Olmsted, and Eliot three hundred dollars for the plan which he received in November 1895. The minimal fee was undoubtedly due to the philanthropic nature of Tufts's project; and except for its smaller scale, the plan resembled other private communities, like Riverside outside Chicago, and Tarrytown Heights just north of New York City, that had been designed by Olmsted.

Within three years, many of Olmsted's ideas for Pinehurst had been implemented. Curvilinear streets were graded, building set-back limitations were established, and the Holly Inn, which over-looked a graceful, tree-lined, New England–like common called the Village Green, was completed and opened for business. For recreation, Tufts included an ample number of croquet and tennis courts as well as a casino. And approximately twenty small cabins, constructed to house Pinehurst's convalescent population, lined streets named "Azalea," "Sycamore," "Magnolia," and "Palmetto."

Before Pinehurst was fully developed, however, Tufts learned that medical science had determined that tuberculosis was a contagious rather than a congenital disease. This proved to be an immediate setback to the development, because if tuberculosis was communicable, it could be treated, and convalescent resorts were sure to become a thing of the past. Out of necessity, Tufts changed the focus of Pinehurst entirely to recreation and introduced several outdoor sports, including golf, which he hoped would attract wealthy northern vacationers in search of a place to spend long winter months.[2]

When James Walker Tufts died in 1902, his only son, Leonard, inherited Pinehurst. Within four years, for reasons that are not altogether clear, Leonard disposed of his father's Boston business interests, and in order to devote full attention to the resort's development, moved his family to North Carolina. By 1906, four hotels were open at Pinehurst: the original Holly Inn, the Magnolia, the Berkshire, and the Carolina; fifty cabins were available for rent; and two golf courses were under construction. Tufts soon realized, however, that if he was to keep these hotels full, and interest visitors in Pinehurst's real estate—which at that time was considered to be in the middle of nowhere—he would have to make the resort more accessible.

The Holly Inn, ca. 1900, overlooking the Village Green, was the first of several hotels opened at the turn of the century in Pinehurst, North Carolina.

The railroad, which Olmsted had incorporated into Pinehurst's design, was the resort's first link to the outside world. But once the automobile age dawned, Tufts had the foresight to promote the concept of automobile tourism to his development. He was very impressed with the success the owners of the Waukewan House, a first-class tourist hotel located on the banks of Lake Winnipesaukee in Meredith, New Hampshire, had had in promoting their resort by improving a four-hundred to five-hundred mile road from New York City straight to the steps of the New England hotel. "The hotel is probably one of the most successful hotels in the North," Tufts wrote in 1909, "and automobiles are going across the road continuously. Oftentimes one hundred or more arrive in a day."

Tufts visited the Waukewan House in 1909, and the success he observed apparently provided him with enough inspiration to want to achieve the same for Pinehurst. In the spring of that same year, he attended a meeting in Richmond, Virginia, of the International League for Highway Improvement where a scheme to build a highway named the "Capital Route" was discussed. According to the plan, the proposed highway would connect the nation's capital with the capitals of Virginia, North Carolina, South Carolina, and Georgia. The idea was in response to the announced automobile reliability contest sponsored by the New York *Herald* and the Atlanta *Journal* between New York and Atlanta in the autumn of 1909. What particularly interested Tufts was that the two sponsoring newspapers proposed to award one thousand dollars to the county having the best stretch of road over which the contestants would travel, and that the route the motorists were to take would link Pinehurst directly with the populous Northeast in the same way that the New Hampshire hotel route had done with New York City.[3]

With the assistance of Dr. E. M. Whaley, president of the Columbia (South Carolina) Automobile Club, and Frank Weldon, publisher of an Atlanta trade journal called the *Railroad Record*, Tufts organized a conference held in Columbia, South Carolina, on 10 June 1909. The purpose of the meeting was to bring together as many representatives as possible of counties, towns, chambers of commerce, and boards of trade located between Atlanta and the

District of Columbia. Instead of taking a westerly course through northeastern Georgia, upstate South Carolina, the North Carolina Piedmont, and western Virginia, Tufts and Weldon wanted the route of the contest to follow the fall line and link, as was proposed earlier, the state capitals of Georgia, South Carolina, North Carolina, and Virginia with Washington. This route, dubbed the "Capital Highway" or "Capital City Route" (see map 1), would pass directly through Pinehurst and accomplish just what Tufts wanted. In promotion of the route, the two businessmen argued that "the sand and clay along our route have a marked binding or cementing quality – or affinity. We are confident that the auto tourists will quickly realize that the Capital highway offers the best route especially in the winter months when the tourists come South by the thousand."

The senate chamber of the South Carolina State House was the scene of the Columbia meeting. It attracted approximately one hundred southerners from Georgia, South Carolina, North Carolina, and Virginia who organized themselves into the Capital Highway Association, elected Leonard Tufts as their president, and pledged to do all they could to convince officials of the Atlanta *Journal* and New York *Herald* that the Capital City Route would be the best for the fall contest. In the weeks following the organizational meeting in Columbia, Tufts spared neither effort nor expense in promotion of the route. After scouting the proposed Capital Highway, however, contest officials selected a more established westerly route which had been first opened a year earlier.[4] This rough automobile road was called the National Highway because in the state of Maryland it covered a small segment of the old 677-mile National Road from Baltimore, Maryland, to Vandalia, Illinois, which the federal government built between 1820 and 1840. (See map 1.)

The argument that the sand-clay roads of the Capital Highway were better for touring than the red clay byways of the National Highway apparently fell on deaf ears. Contest officials were immensely impressed by the enthusiasm and cordiality shown by chamber of commerce representatives from cities like Greensboro, Charlotte, Spartanburg, and Anderson – through which the National Highway passed – who greeted their scout cars when they

Map 1. National Highway, New York to Atlanta, 1909; Capital Highway, Washington to Atlanta, 1910.

surveyed the route. Capital Highway Association officials, on the other hand, did not have much success in arousing support for the reliability run through the rural counties and small towns through which the Capital Route passed. The short time period in which highway officials had to organize welcoming parties and convince rural southerners that the route would benefit their communities worked against them; but Leonard Tufts and his associates had an additional obstacle to overcome.

Unlike midwesterners, farmers in the South in 1909 still disliked and distrusted the noisy, citified automobiles that frightened their livestock, tore up their dirt roads, and sometimes damaged their property. The Columbia *State* newspaper, which unhesitatingly supported the Capital Highway, carried an editorial in June 1909 that addressed the problem. "The farmer . . . in the great Midwest," the South Carolina paper stated,

> has put the motor car to the test in so many ways that its advantage as an adjunct to his means of obtaining a livelihood is absolutely certain. This road [the Capital Highway], then, would for one thing familiarize the farmer with the motor car and popularize it. For years a prejudice against the automobile has existed in the country's districts, due largely to uncertain reckless and unscrupulous drivers.[5]

The Capital Highway Association was unable to change, or even hide, these feelings on the part of farmers in the South before the route selection committee made its decision on the course of the 1909 race. The reliability run, therefore, did not link Pinehurst with the capitals of Virginia, North Carolina, and Georgia as Leonard Tufts had hoped. But while Tufts and his vanguard Capital Highway Association—the first of its kind in the South—failed in their immediate objective, they contributed greatly to a new understanding of what an axial highway connecting the South with the North could mean.

Over the next four years, between 1909 and 1913, the American Automobile Association (AAA) took the lead in promoting interstate highway construction in the South. In 1910, the AAA sponsored a reliability run which began in Cincinnati and, after winding through six southern states, terminated in Chicago. The following year, Charles J. Glidden, the Boston millionaire and automobile enthusiast who, since 1905, had conducted highly publicized motoring tours throughout the country for AAA members, came into the South for the first time. The grueling event he sponsored began in New York City, followed the National Highway to Atlanta, and concluded in Jacksonville, Florida. Fifty cars and several hundred men and women from the South, including Georgia Governor Hoke

Smith, participated in the 1911 contest. That same year, AAA executives organized the American Road Congress to promote the motor world's idea of interstate highway construction. At the organizational meeting in Richmond, Virginia, which featured President William Howard Taft as a speaker, AAA delegates from across the nation gathered to discuss a variety of highway topics, including the construction of a route between the North and South. The next year, 1912, A. G. Batchelder, chairman of the executive committee of the AAA, addressed the annual meeting of the North Carolina Good Roads Association. He told the audience that "a long stretch of improved road is one of the best advertisements

After a few days of inclement weather, one of the pathfinding vehicles of the 1911 Glidden Tour, which came as far south as Jacksonville, Florida, found the going tough and had to be pried from the mud by helpful bystanders.

a state can have. It changes by the sheer force of publicity," he said, "backward localities into progressive ones, enhances [land] values, and brings into general notice resources which before had been only locally known."[6]

All of these events stimulated southerners' imagination and stirred up a strong sentiment for highway construction. By 1913, therefore, when one of the leading proponents of commerce and industrial development in the South publicly advocated the construction of a north-south highway, it was not totally unexpected. On the front page of its 25 September 1913 issue, the *Manufacturers Record* first outlined the story of the proposed Lincoln Highway, a ten-million-dollar east-west project planned to connect New York City with San Francisco via Pittsburgh, Indianapolis, Chicago, Omaha, and Salt Lake City. The Lincoln Highway Association had been organized in Indianapolis in October 1912, and large contributions from northern companies like the Prest-O-Lite Battery Company, the Goodyear Tire and Rubber Company, and the Hudson Motor Car Company—each of which had much to gain from the construction of long interstate tourist highways—helped get the enormous project started. "There is another highway," the weekly newspaper continued, that is "equally as important—indeed, we believe far more important—that demands the energetic co-operation of the business interests of the North and West in connection with those in the South." Editors of the *Record* stated their awareness of the existing National Highway connecting the Northeast and the South but concluded that, because the route was for the most part unpaved and impassible in winter and spring months, it was almost totally inadequate. "Something far more comprehensive is needed," the *Record* told its readers. "The highway demanded by the times is one unbroken line from the North and the West through the South." The *Record* justified its opinion by stating that the proposed highway would make possible material developments and an increase in business interests between the North and South and the West which promised to make it worth many times its cost.[7]

Within a week, letters of approval from across the South poured into the *Record*'s Baltimore office. "Your proposal," wrote Howard H. Stafford, president of the Georgia-Carolina Brick Company of Augusta, Georgia, "would bring about a more immediate association between the people of the North and South." Clopton Thomas, secretary of the Corinth, Mississippi, Business Men's Club, wrote that the suggestion so impressed him that he planned to bring the matter before the club's board of directors for their approval. And the Atlanta *Journal* commented editorially that such a direct link

Glidden tourists in November 1911 assemble on Peachtree Road, just north of the Atlanta city limits, before making a triumphal drive downtown. Among the dignitaries who made the eight-hundred-fifty-mile trek from New York was Georgia governor Hoke Smith. Courtesy of the Georgia Department of Archives and History, Brown/Connally/Spalding Collection (AC 00–076).

with the North "would quicken industry and enrich commerce beyond measure."[8]

Everyone agreed that the highway should be built. The South's business community enthusiastically endorsed the idea as if it were an inspiration. But proponents of this suggestion had the same problem that the earlier generation of good roads advocates had: who was going to pay for it? Large corporate donations had helped fund the initial stages of the Lincoln Highway's development, but no such commitment was forthcoming from northern industry to help get a north-south highway started. Northern business leaders even those in automobile manufacturing and related industries, were not yet convinced that a direct link with the South would mean a boost to their businesses. They still viewed the South more as a supplier of natural resources and raw materials to fuel the demands of the North's industrial economy than as a marketplace in which expensive industrial products, like automobiles, could be sold successfully.

Carl Graham Fisher was an exception to this rule, and for good reason. He had more at stake than mere profits. As founder of the Prest-O-Lite Battery Company – which manufactured carbide battery–powered headlights for automobiles, enabling motorists for the first time to drive after dark – and as an organizer of the Indianapolis Speedway, Fisher had made a fortune. By 1913, however, he had invested heavily in Florida real estate, and like Leonard Tufts at Pinehurst, realized that he needed a way to get potential buyers to Florida.

In 1910, when he and his wife visited the sleepy tropical village of Miami on their honeymoon, Fisher, who was forever hatching colossal schemes for making money, became interested in purchasing some property in south Florida. A year or so later, he bought a house on Biscayne Bay and began to spend his winters there. On one visit, he met John Stiles Collins, a seventy-five-year-old retired New Jersey horticulturist, who owned sixteen hundred acres on Miami Beach. Collins had tried unsuccessfully to grow both coconuts and avocados there and explained to the Indianan that he was hoping to develop the beach front as a residential area. By then Fisher had sold the Prest-O-Lite Company to the Union Carbide Corporation for nine million dollars and was looking for new investment opportunities. "I like to see things grow," he once remarked, "I want to build things. . . . I want to get things done." After checking with Frank Shutts, a Miami attorney who represented railroad entrepreneur Henry Flagler, Fisher decided to lend Collins fifty thousand dollars so that a two-and-a-half-mile wooden bridge could be completed across Biscayne Bay, uniting the Florida mainland with the sixteen hundred acres on Miami Beach. In return, Fisher received bonds on the bridge, an eighteen-hundred-foot-wide strip of land running across the heart of the tropical peninsula from Biscayne Bay to the Atlantic Ocean, and the option of purchasing an additional two hundred acres of beachfront property at a later date.

Fisher had entered the real estate business, and having earlier conceived the Lincoln Highway, which stretched from Atlantic to Pacific, his motives went unquestioned when he proposed a similar route linking the North and the South. His idea first appeared in the Indianapolis *News*, and as he had done with Packard Motor Car Company President Henry B. Joy in promotion of the Lincoln Highway, Fisher was shrewd enough to allow his Hoosier colleague, William S. Gilbreath, to take the lead in the advancement of the new north-south highway. In the meantime, Fisher stayed in Miami Beach, where an army of workers hacked away miles of mangrove and huge cranes dredged artificial islands out of Biscayne Bay.[9]

In November 1914, Gilbreath went to Atlanta to attend the fourth annual meeting of the American Road Congress. Carrying a letter from Indiana Governor Samuel M. Ralston endorsing the proposed north-south highway, Gilbreath met with Georgia Governor John M. Slaton, who also gave his support to the project. Gilbreath said he was trying to gain the approval of the governors of all the states through which the proposed route would pass, but he also knew that if the highway was ever to become a reality he needed the enthusiastic endorsement of southerners as well. Therefore, in an article that appeared on the front page of the Atlanta *Constitution* on 10 November 1914, Gilbreath broke the news of the proposed interstate route and told southerners for the first time what they could expect once the highway was completed. He called the road the "Cotton Belt Route" but noted that the people of the South could rename it if they so desired. He advised his readers that the outbreak of war in Europe would prohibit Americans in the years to come from traveling abroad and said that he believed it was a good time to form an organization to oversee construction of the north-south highway. "You people in the South," he went on,

> have wonderful scenery that is most unusual and attractive to owners of automobiles in the middle western states, and we are only waiting for an opportunity to drive through your country. I understand from road guides that sections [of the existing National Highway] are not first class, while other parts are unusually bad. It is this lack of a thoroughly connected highway leading through the South which discourages tourists. I think . . . 300,000 automobile tourists would use this road this winter [1914–15].

Southerners had heard all this before, but Gilbreath concluded his pitch with an extremely optimistic estimate of the potential profits the South could expect to realize once the highway opened for traffic. The average car, he said, contained four persons who each spent an average of five dollars each day on food, hotels, gasoline, and tires. This meant that, if the estimated 300,000 automobiles traveled over the highway during the winter, each day they were in the South six million dollars would change hands from northerner to southerner. "It does not take a great deal of figuring," Gilbreath added, "to see the immense amount of money that would be left in the southern states by an invasion of this class of desirable people."[10]

For the next four months Gilbreath traveled in Georgia, Tennessee, and Kentucky, promoting Fisher's idea. He addressed Rotarians, business leaders' associations, and local automobile clubs, whose members all found his logic tantalizing. By 3 April 1915, when Indiana Governor Ralston and Tennessee Governor Tom C. Rye called a highway organizational meeting in Chattanooga, southerners had renamed the proposed route the "Dixie Highway" and had become so agitated with anticipation over the prospect of the highway coming through their particular communities that a monumental struggle ensued. Business leaders and politicians from over one hundred communities throughout Illinois, Ohio, Indiana, Kentucky, Tennessee, Georgia, and Florida converged on the Tennessee city and waged a propaganda war later referred to as the "Second Battle of Chattanooga." Counties that for years had procrastinated in the improvement of their roads were presented at this meeting as progressive, forward-looking communities with magnificent public road systems. This aggrandizement came not only from large cities like Atlanta, long known for its successive booster campaigns, but from smaller towns and communities not yet proficient in the art of self-promotion. So eager were southerners to have their town or county on the Dixie Highway map that, when a delegate rose from his seat at the Chattanooga meeting to proclaim the merits of his community, representatives from rival communities hurled insults and taunting criticisms at him.

The desire of so many communities to have the route pass through their town or county, in addition to the heckling and lack of order at the April meeting, prevented the establishment of an official route for the highway. However, an organization called the "Dixie Highway Association" was formed; Gilbreath was named field secretary; and Michael Morrison Allison, an articulate Tennessee circuit judge and Chattanooga attorney personally familiar with the tribulations of travel over unimproved roads in the South, was elected president. To settle the controversy of where the highway would finally pass, the governors of the seven states represented at the April meeting in Chattanooga agreed to appoint two delegates or commissioners from their respective states to serve on a route selection commission. Once the commission had been established, it was agreed that the fourteen commissioners would hold a second meeting in Chattanooga in May and, after listening to arguments from competing communities, decide on the official course of the route.[11]

Weeks before this all-important meeting was held, however, southerners busied themselves demonstrating how much they wanted the highway. Some counties, like McCreary County, Kentucky, which had not done the first thing in the way of road improvements, suddenly got busy pushing dirt around to give the appearance, at least, that good roads were a priority. In three Georgia counties – Walker, Chattooga, and Floyd – new bridge construction began, local politicians introduced new road improvement legislation, and interested citizens filled potholes and smoothed bad places in their existing roads. These activities were, of course, advertisements to attract the highway, but they prompted the Chattanooga *Times* to remark editorially that the time when a "mossback [Tennessean] can defeat good roads legislation by simply shouting, 'Vote 'er down, boys!'" had finally passed, and that a new era of transportation development was dawning.[12]

The 20 May 1915 meeting of the route selection committee of the Dixie Highway Association proceeded with much greater order than had the organizational meeting a month earlier. Atlanta newspaperman Clark Howell, who chaired the route selection commission, arranged a two-day schedule to hear presentations from various communities in competition for the highway. Before a final route determination could be made, however, a controversy between Howell and Carl Fisher erupted. Fisher placed such importance on a satisfactory settlement of the highway's official course that he left his Miami Beach real estate development long enough to represent his home state of Indiana on the conclusive selection committee. Fisher naturally wanted an immediate designation of the route and locked horns with Howell, who felt that the decision should be postponed. Fisher argued that enthusiasm for the highway would wane if a definite course was not decided upon as soon as possible. Howell, on the other hand, favored a more competitive approach. He was of the opinion that the highway would be built faster if competing counties went ahead and constructed their portion of the route. Once completed, he proposed that the merits of these short county roads would determine which direction through the South the Dixie Highway would finally take.

But Fisher needed a route constructed to his emerging Miami real estate development without delay, and he managed to persuade enough members of the selection committee to override Howell's more practical proposal. On 22 May, the committee met in private

Map 2. Dixie Highway, Eastern and Western routes, Sault Sainte Marie, Michigan, to Miami, Florida, 1918.

session to make its final decision. After five hours of deliberation, Howell emerged from a smoke-filled assembly room of the Hamilton County Court House and, to the surprise of everyone, announced that the Dixie Highway would not be one continuously paved road linking the Midwest with the South after all. Instead, he stated that two highways, measuring a total of 3,989 miles, with an eastern and western division, were the official plan. (See map 2.) The committee had obviously felt the pressure from the warring constituencies at the Chattanooga meeting. Fearing that the rejection of one group might ultimately jeopardize the success of the highway, committee members had once again listened to the reasoning of Carl Fisher, who suggested the compromise. The eastern part of the route was planned to pass through Cincinnati and Knoxville, the western part through Louisville and Nashville. All four of these cities had strong, influential delegations at the second Chattanooga meeting, and the dual highway was the best way to satisfy the greatest number of people.

Within two years of Howell's announcement, several changes had been made in the Dixie Highway's official course. In 1916 the association granted Michigan admission to the organization, and promoters then claimed that the route linked two of the most remote and culturally different places in the country: Sault Sainte Marie, Michigan, and Miami Beach, Florida. In addition, a leg of the highway extending east from Knoxville over the Smoky Mountains to Asheville, North Carolina, south through the South Carolina Piedmont and Low Country to Savannah, and on to Jacksonville was added. The Dixie Highway had evolved from a single route envisioned to link the North and South into a complicated network of roads that passed through ten states.[13]

To southerners the prospect of having their communities literally put on the map by this highway represented a rare opportunity to cash in on the projected tourist bonanza. To Carl Fisher, on the other hand, who made certain that he was included in the critical planning phase of the highway, the road potentially meant millions. Before the Dixie Highway Association began to promote the road through its official publication, *Dixie Highway*, mark the route with red and white signs bearing the letters "DH," act as a tourist bureau for northern automobilists who wanted to drive south, and solicit construction funds from southerners, Fisher's Miami Beach land development was anything but a success. But once the route was announced to pass through more northern industrial cities—like Detroit, Chicago, Cincinnati, Dayton, Indianapolis, and Toledo—than a single highway could possibly have done, Miami Beach came to life. Fisher did not exploit the South in the same way as other

Dixie Highway magazine, published by the Dixie Highway Association, often featured stories about Florida and illustrations, like this November 1918 front cover, promoting the state as a veritable paradise.

northern industrialists who treated the region as a colonial economy to be robbed of its natural resources. He carefully and cleverly manipulated ambitious southern business leaders by showing them a way to earn the profits they had always wanted. Then the transplanted Indianan sat back and waited while they literally built a highway to his doorstep. Fisher never spent a dime to build the Dixie Highway; all he did was promote it. In 1915 he incorporated the city of Miami, and over the next decade he greeted thousands of midwesterners who drove south to visit Miami Beach and to buy a piece of Florida sunshine.

At the conclusion of the 1920s, southerners were still at work improving the last remaining stretches of the Dixie Highway. Completion of the project was slow because it involved the coordinated efforts of more than fifty counties in ten states. State and county bond issues and federal subsidies, along with local contributions from owners of hotels, restaurants, and automotive supply stores along the route, paid for the highway. And, while mountains often hindered construction, politics proved to be an even more cumbersome obstacle. Michael Morrison Allison, president of the Dixie Highway Association, spent most of his time as fund-raiser and lobbyist for the highway. On more than one occasion he became so infuriated by state legislatures' failure to appropriate the funds necessary to build sections of the route that he threatened to resign.[14]

Allison's frustration stemmed from state legislators and county commissioners having no interest in subsidizing a highway that would not pass through their communities and from which they would derive little benefit. Lawmakers from western Tennessee, for example, were reluctant to authorize funds that would only pay to have permanent roads within the state joined to form links with the Dixie Highway, let alone appropriate money to help pay for the entire project. After 1916, when federal funds for the first time became available to state highway departments across the South, this same attitude persisted in Tennessee, as the state's ninety-six counties competed with one another for the money rather than work together to get the Dixie Highway completed. Once the United

States entered World War I, however, Dixie Highway officials gained an advantage. They argued tirelessly that the interstate route should receive priority funding because it connected the numerous military camps scattered throughout the South with the rest of the nation and thereby improved national security.[15]

The delay in having a uniformly paved highway linking the Midwest and the South was due also to competition from rival highway associations. The publicity Carl Fisher and his promoters gave the Dixie Highway prompted other highway progressives to want to get in on the action. By starting highway associations of their own, these individuals, who espoused all the good roads rhetoric, hoped to cash in on the expected tourist windfall. Between 1915 and 1920, hundreds of new interstate highway associations were formed throughout the South. Invariably, the routes these organizations promoted began in other parts of the country and, like the Dixie Highway, connected places as remote as Sault Sainte Marie, Michigan, with the South. Five of the most publicized of these routes were the Andrew Jackson Highway, which connected Chicago with New Orleans via Mobile, Alabama; the Robert E. Lee Highway, which linked the northeastern United States with San Francisco by way of seven southern states; the John H. Bankhead National Highway, which connected the District of Columbia with San Diego and Los Angeles; the Jefferson Davis National Highway, which also stretched across the southern United States between Washington and San Francisco; and the Dixie Overland Highway, which put Savannah, Georgia, and the Deep South in closer touch with the West Coast and the cities of San Diego, Los Angeles, and San Francisco. (See maps 3 and 4.)

Less publicized interstate highways like the Cincinnati–Lookout Mountain–Air–Line Route, the Scenic Tourist Highway, the Chattanooga–Gadsden–Birmingham–Lookout Mountain Scenic Highway, the Ozark Trail, and the Mississippi River Scenic Highway also began to appear in automobile guidebooks and road maps of the South. In addition, shorter in-state roads like the Paris-Houston Highway in Texas and the Tamiami Trail between Tampa and Miami, Florida, added even more highways to the growing list of

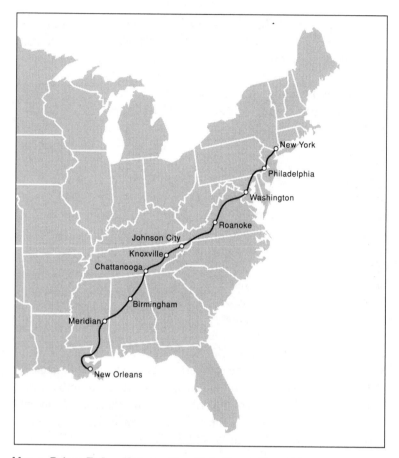

Map 3. Robert E. Lee Highway, New York City to New Orleans, 1921.

routes in the South that competed for funds. In Texas alone, thirty-eight in-state highways could be found on any 1922 road map of the state. By 1924, so much confusion existed from all these private highways, which crisscrossed and overlapped one another, that the American Association of State Highway Officials persuaded the secretary of agriculture to appoint an official board to sort out the confusion. The Joint Board of State and Federal Highway Officials designated which routes would be federal in-

Map 4. John H. Bankhead National Highway, Washington to San Diego, California, 1921.

terstate highways and worked out a uniform system of numbering and marking. East-west routes were given even numbers and those running north and south odd numbers. In addition, federal interstate highways were marked with black-and-white shields that specified each highway's number.[16]

But the question of how these roads were to be improved remained. And did they, in actuality, serve the needs of the people in the communities through which they passed? These and other questions became important considerations not only to governmental policymakers who decided how highway funds would be distributed but to farmers who had seen their interests pushed aside by highway progressives who understood profits and progress to be one and the same.

Highway promoters did not ignore farmers like they did farm issues. But despite reconciliatory efforts by those interested in linking the North or Midwest with the South, or any two points in between, farmers still felt abandoned by the good roads movement and its new leadership. When highway progressives implored farmers to join them in the good roads fraternity, they were really asking them to support a cause that theoretically benefited everyone but practically only served the interests of automobile tourists, merchants, real estate investors, and members of the business community. In addition to attracting out-of-state tourists, interstate highways brought a new source of revenue to the South and, at the same time, reduced distribution costs. This made possible the receipt of a wider variety of consumer goods which could be offered for sale in stores throughout the region. Upwardly mobile southerners found this greatly beneficial to their increasing affluence, but many farmers did not; and when the excitement about the construction of tourist highways began, the apathy farmers had traditionally shown toward good roads turned to resentment and finally to outspoken criticism.

As early as 1911, the federal government classified public roads as either trunk-line highways, like the Capital Highway, which ran for long distances and connected towns and cities along the way, or farm-to-market roads, which radiated from market towns and shipping stations and covered much shorter distances. Highway progressives in the South tried to convince skeptical farmers that trunk-line highway construction would generate the improvement of these shorter in-state roads which, they argued, would be built to connect farms with trunk-line roads at strategic towns and cities. The highway, in other words, was to be the catalyst for future road improvements. Farmers, however, were not at all sold on this idea and did not like having their needs made subordinate to those of urban merchants. Farmers argued that, by giving attention first to farm towns and shipping stations, and later, as additional funds became available, extending road improvements out into the countryside, entire regions in a matter of a few years would be covered by intricate road networks. Then by connecting adjoining road systems, they concluded, trunk-lines would be formed automatically.[17]

The potential for profits over interstate highways leading into the South was far too great an enticement to business leaders for them to do anything more than listen to farmers' criticisms of their highway plans. As a result, farmers became more outspoken. In September 1913, C. O. Raine, an official of the Missouri Grange, sent a letter to Grange members in which he proclaimed that "federal aid should not stop with cross State Highways, but should extend down to the township roads." A month later, the *Journal of Agriculture and Star Farmer* called farmers' attention to a good roads convention to be held in November in St. Louis. "Farmers by the thousand should be present," the journal stated,

> to impress upon the convention the supreme importance of the local farm road as compared with boulevards and so-called highways. [The good roads convention] will be an excellent opportunity to make their attitude toward roads known. They can show that they are not opposed to fine boulevards, but consider them of secondary importance to the farm roads. The farm road should receive first attention, and after that the boulevard, instead of the present custom of spending large sums on a few boulevards and neglecting the farm roads entirely. The farmers' needs in good roads should be made clear.[18]

A year later at the forty-eighth annual convention of the National Grange, in Wilmington, Delaware, a special committee on highways made the position of farmers clear. The committee reported that there was "Great Danger" in the diversion of good roads sentiment "toward the construction of scenic highways." Using familiar farmer logic that the first roads to be given attention should be those that put producers in closer touch with consumers and help to reduce the costs of hauling farm products to market, the special committee concluded its objections to the good roads movement policy in 1914 by insisting that road construction "be kept within the smallest possible unit of population . . . in order that the money appropriated . . . be spent close to the people most directly concerned."

In keeping with these considerations, the Grange adopted six resolutions, the most poignant of which attacked the willingness of highway advocates to have states assume large debts in the form of bond issues to pay for interstate tourist routes. This struck at the very heart of highway progressives' ability to accomplish their objectives. "We are opposed to the many binding schemes advanced by those seeking touring roads," the second resolution read, "believing that the pay-as-you-go policy is far more business-like." The sixth and final resolution encouraged local committees of farmers to lobby against any state or local road building measures that would not serve farmers' interests first and foremost.[19]

The negative reaction of farmers to the construction of interstate tourist highways is unmistakable evidence of how lost the basic progressive ideals of the good roads movement eventually became. While the label "progressive" may very well pertain to road improvement efforts in the South aimed at improving education, increasing church attendance, facilitating farmers' efforts to get their produce to market, and helping to reduce expensive railroad rates, it does not accurately apply to what the movement actually became: an effort to construct long-distance interstate highways. The good roads movement was at first an extension of populist demands and a part of a more widespread campaign in the South to address the region's social, economic, and cultural backwardness. Although the movement had goals as forward-looking as any other reform issue of its time, theory was about as far as efforts went to enhance farm life in the South. Those who advocated road improvements to address rural concerns were simply unable to transform their convictions, persuasive as they were, into actual accomplishments. The unwillingness of farmers—the main beneficiaries of public road improvements—to pay taxes in support of better roads was partly responsible for this failure by preventing the statute labor system from being overhauled and hindering reformers' efforts to raise road revenues via bonded indebtedness. But also to blame were good roads reformers themselves who did not relate their progressive ideas for a better South through road improvements to a broad enough segment of the population.

In the final analysis, the original aim of the good roads movement in the South to rejuvenate agriculture and stimulate rural development was a progressive theory that never saw fruition. Perhaps if farmers had not been so reluctant to shoulder some, if not all, of the financial burden necessary to have better roads, New South business interests would not have so easily become the focus of the movement. By continually opposing taxation, farmers put themselves in a conservative and defensive position which never changed. They continually opposed any form of indebtedness to pay for road construction and insisted that government appropriations for road building be kept to a minimum and at the local level. Highway progressives, on the other hand, constantly sought government support for the construction and maintenance of long-distance tourist highways and lobbied relentlessly for the passage of deficit-spending measures to pay for the routes, whether in-state or interstate, that they envisioned. The road building and improvement undertaken in Florida during the gubernatorial administrations of Sidney J. Catts (1917–21) and John W. Martin (1925–29) and in North Carolina by governors Locke Craig (1913–17) and Cameron Morrison (1921–26) were, by and large, the results of the arguments used to promote this brand of progressivism.[20]

Farmers never offered any alternative spending proposals, and their conservatism undoubtedly caused many southerners both to lose interest in the broader more far-reaching reform objectives of the good roads movement and to listen more intently to highway progressives who argued for road improvements in the name of economic development. This made it easy for business interests in the South, as far as the good roads movement went, to take control.

As good roads proponents, highway progressives were never able to enlist the support of the majority of farmers in the movement once it changed its focus. By selling the idea of good roads for economic betterment, however, these same highway promoters were successful in their appeal to the growing contingent of middle-class southerners. In other regions of the United States, progressivism was understood to stand for reform; but in the South, at least when the issue was good roads, progressivism meant economic development. The highway movement in the South succeeded while the farm-to-market road movement failed because business leaders, who fashioned themselves as highway progressives, convinced many southerners that modernization was tangibly intertwined with the construction of long-distance tourist routes. Unlike farm-to-market roads, highways brought new jobs, new business opportunities, and new investments to the South. This was Progress with a capital *P*, the kind that no southerner interested in greater economic opportunity could ignore.

3

John Asa Rountree and the
United States Good Roads Association

The proliferation of highway associations in the South between 1910 and 1920 promoting both intrastate and interstate tourist highways, as we have seen, gave rise to a great deal of competition for public recognition as well as for the limited funds the federal government was slowly beginning to make available to state governments. One astute southerner who had been associated with the grass-roots good roads movement in Alabama for many years saw an opportunity to exploit this growing competitiveness and earn a reputation for himself as a civic-minded, forward-looking progressive businessman.

John Asa Rountree was an avuncular, middle-aged, Birmingham publisher who was no novice when it came either to the issue of good roads or to Alabama politics. He argued that the competition between highway associations and disgruntled farmers was counterproductive to the South's chances for self-improvement. In 1913, after distinguishing himself as a high-ranking member of the Democratic Party of Alabama, Rountree formed the United States Good Roads Association (USGRA). This was the most comprehensive good roads association ever organized in the South, and its purpose was to advance both the individual objectives of highway associations and the goals of those who favored road improvements in impoverished rural areas where accessibility to markets was extremely limited.

The success of the USGRA was a tribute to the inventiveness

and promotional skill of Rountree, but it is also a testament to the convoluted nature of southern progressivism. Rountree's career as a good roads advocate shows both the transition of the movement from populist to progressive and how the issue of good roads in the South lost whatever reform identity it had and became the property of highway progressives. Rountree eventually joined the ranks of these highway progressives and manipulated his long-cultivated reform image to benefit both himself and his good roads organization. He was a quintessential example of the group of southerners at this time who, as Sheldon Hackney put it, sought to achieve "Hamiltonian ends with Jeffersonian means."[1]

Asa Rountree was born on 23 March 1867, when much of the South lay in ruins from the ravages of the Civil War, and in a part of the region, Morgan County, Alabama, which many people still considered backcountry. He was the second of twelve children born to Dr. Scott L. Rountree, a Confederate Army surgeon who returned to Morgan County following the war and, near what would soon become the small town of Hartselle, started a medical practice.

Rountree and Hartselle grew up together. After 1872, when the North and South Alabama Railroad extended its tracks through Morgan County, Hartselle became a station from which lumber and farm products were shipped out of the lower Tennessee Valley. By the time Rountree was in his teens, new residents had started new businesses and built new homes and churches, putting Hartselle on the map for the first time. One of the first businesses to legitimize the small town's existence was a local newspaper, the *Investigator*, which began publication in 1871. Rountree took an early interest in journalism and, at the age of fourteen, worked as a reporter for the *Investigator*. By the time he was twenty, and after several years of working as a correspondent for other publications in and around Morgan County, Rountree rose to the position of editor, publisher, and part-owner of the *Investigator*, whose name he changed to the *Alabama Enquirer*.[2]

Rountree began his career as editor and publisher of the *Enquirer* on a note that sounded very much like his big-city contem-

John Asa Rountree (1867–1936) at work in his Birmingham, Alabama, office, ca. 1917. Rountree was director general of both the United States Good Roads Association and the Bankhead National Highway Association. Courtesy of the Birmingham Public Library, Archives Division.

porary, Henry W. Grady. "It is natural," he wrote on 7 July 1887, "that northern capital should seek a safe and profitable investment. Attracted by the marvelous growth and development of the south, it is coming of its own volition . . . to aid in the upbuilding of a section which offers capitalists superior inducements for safe and secure returns upon their investments."[3] His boosterism, however, soon gave way to a more populist point of view. This was due to the growing unrest among farmers in northern Alabama, who, like farmers elsewhere, were shackled with agricultural surpluses, low prices, and a crop mortgage system which kept them constantly in debt.

Dirt-poor and frustrated by what seemed to be an inability to do anything about it, during the 1880s farmers across the South listened more closely to the dissident populist rhetoric of the times, which called for freeing farmers from debt, restoring the nation to a cash basis, and bringing prosperity to working-class Americans. In the mid-1880s, Morgan County was a stronghold of populism, having five active Grange chapters alone. The Patrons of Husbandry, however, were soon outnumbered by members of two other farm organizations: the Agricultural Wheel and the Farmers' Alliance and Cooperative Union. C. W. Macune, organizer and first president of the original Farmers' Alliance in east Texas, was eager to spread his message to other southern states and, in 1887, the year Rountree took over the *Enquirer*, dispatched six Alliance disciples to Alabama. In March, one of these men, lecturer A. T. Jacobson, organized the first Alliance chapter in the state in Madison County, located just across the Tennessee River adjacent to Morgan County. Within a matter of months, sub-Alliances sprang up throughout northern Alabama, but particularly in the Sixth and Seventh Congressional Districts.[4]

All of this unrest did not go unnoticed by Rountree and his newspaper. Over a period of about eighteen months, the *Enquirer* began to soft-pedal its New South booster rhetoric and, instead, to echo the concerns of farmers who lived in Morgan County and neighboring counties. Although he vehemently opposed the ideas of the politically oriented Agricultural Wheel, Rountree supported most of the reform ideology he heard his farmer neighbors voicing. On 29 March 1888, he wrote that southerners "have far too long produced and sent to the north goods to be manufactured, and then returned to us at five hundred per cent additional cost." His solution was for southerners to manufacture their own clothes, stoves, plows, wagons, bedsteads, tables, washing machines, and corn shellers and then send them to the North for sale. Two years later, when Alliance membership in Alabama increased to between 120,000 and 125,000, with three thousand sub-Alliance lodges throughout the state, and when Alliance men wielded substantial political power in the state legislature, Rountree fully committed the viewpoint of his paper to farming interests. "The agricultural and laboring class," he wrote on 18 June 1891, "have found out that they have not received and are not receiving their share of the fruits of their labor. They mean to have a chance in the methods of distribution." He called the Alliance "a great social movement" and stated that there was but one way to "stay the progress of the farm movement" and that was to "redress the grievances of the oppressed farmers." For several years thereafter, each weekly issue of the *Enquirer* carried a front-page "Alliance Notes" column keeping local readers abreast of farm issues elsewhere in the South and the nation. By 1892, Rountree referred to his newspaper as an official voice of the Farmers' Alliance in northern Alabama and had made farm reform an editorial priority.[5]

Like approximately one hundred Alabama reform newspapers of its day, the *Enquirer* played a valuable role in promoting and publicizing the ideals of northern Alabama farmers. Populism itself, however, was far too radical for the young Morgan County editor, who, rather than become personally associated with the farm movement, felt more comfortable within the ranks of the Democratic Party. In 1890, Rountree ran for a seat on the Morgan County Democratic Executive Committee, the county policy-making board of the state Democratic Party, and won. As a Democrat with populist leanings, Rountree sympathized with farmers, but their inflammatory rhetoric and socially divisive notions prevented him from actively supporting political candidates like Ruben F. Kolb, a pioneer in the organization of the Alabama Alliance. Once again, Rountree altered the editorial viewpoint of his newspaper, this time in support of the Democratic Party, which was losing much of its membership to Populism. Talk of forming an alternative political party that would be more responsive to the needs of farmers was anathema to him. "The true farmers' party," he wrote emphatically on 23 July 1891, "is the Democratic Party, and the interests of agriculture will be best promoted by putting that party in control of government."[6]

At a time when many of the other reform newspapers in Alabama were having difficulty attracting advertisements from businesses and collecting subscription fees from debt-stricken farmers, Rountree was able to stay in business with little difficulty. His close connection with the Democratic Party and his moderate rather than radical editorial point of view undoubtedly had much to do with this. By 1896, the *Enquirer* carried few Populist endorsements and

had evolved into a strong supporter of the Democratic Party of
Alabama and its political candidates. That same year, Rountree
rose in the ranks of the party to sit on the state Democratic Executive Committee, sold his interest in the Hartselle paper, and
moved to Birmingham, where he purchased a share in the Age-
Herald Publishing Company, publisher of the decidedly Democratic
daily newspaper, the Birmingham *Age-Herald*. Within a few months,
he was in full control of the company, having been elected president and general manager, quite an accomplishment for a twenty-
nine-year-old small-town newspaper publisher who, not so many
years before, had sung the praises of Populism.[7]

Rountree, however, neither abandoned his populist notions
altogether nor embraced bourbonism. Instead, as a businessman
and upstanding member of the Democratic Party of Alabama, he
found he could combine the ideals of a reformer with the profit-
mindedness of a proponent of the New South. He believed that
change could take place in the South by avoiding extreme measures
and by adopting a solid program of economic and commercial
development. In 1896, Rountree stumped the state on behalf of
Joseph F. Johnston, a gubernatorial candidate described by his contemporaries as a "half-way Populist." Johnston, a Birmingham
banker and industrialist, was a New South democrat who appealed
to Alabama voters in 1896 on a platform of free silver, railroad reform, honesty in government, and the establishment of statewide
primary elections. His election and subsequent two terms in office
(1896–1900) were a time when Rountree assumed a prominent
role within the Democratic Party of Alabama and when some progressive gains, like the organization of one of the South's first good
roads association, resulted.

The North Alabama Good Roads Association was organized in
the area of the state where agrarian unrest had been greatest for
more than a decade. It was a manifestation of the progressive gubernatorial administration of Joseph F. Johnston, who, in his first in-
augural address to the state legislature in December 1896, described
the public roads of Alabama as "a disgrace to the commonwealth

and to our civilization." Johnston acknowledged that a few counties had built roads that had increased land values and saved farmers thousands of dollars in hauling costs but held that these counties were the exception and, for matters to improve, competent road engineers would have to be hired, antiquated road laws changed, and—to procure the necessary road maintenance equipment—special taxes levied.[8]

The governor's desire to have the public roads of his state improved was far more than a mere populist impulse on his part. Johnston was a shrewd politician who saw many Alabamians leaving the Democratic Party over the issue of free silver, and who clearly understood that good roads were an issue that the most extreme Populist and the most conservative Democrat could mutually support. The question of better-built public thoroughfares emerged during Johnston's administration, then, for several reasons. First, railroad reformers had been frustrated for a long time in their attempt to regulate the monopolistic railroads effectively and were beginning to recognize that good roads could provide the necessary competition to reduce freight rates. Second, farmers viewed road improvements, as we have seen, as a way of improving their livelihoods and as a chance for a brighter future. Third, New South promoters perceived better roads as a way of modernizing their region and of improving its traditionally backward image. Finally, and most significantly, good roads, like improvements in education and public health, were a political issue with which few were willing to argue. Good roads were, in fact, an issue of both progress and unity. It was no accident that, during Johnston's first term of office, when the state legislature failed on two occasions to pass a law that would have established a centralized system of roads paid for out of state rather than local coffers, the North Alabama Good Roads Association was born.

In his reelection campaign during the summer of 1898, Governor Johnston continued to seek to unify the Democratic Party of Alabama, which remained badly split, mainly over the issue of free silver. Liberal Democrats and Populists accused Johnston of being soft on the silver issue, and as he and other party stalwarts like Oscar Underwood, John H. Bankhead, and Rountree traveled around the state seeking votes, they tried to avoid the divisive silver issue and focus on unifying issues like good roads. Johnston wanted to show his rural constituency that his administration had not sold them out and that he had their interests as a priority. "I showed them," he remarked in July, after a long campaign swing through the state, "how their state officials have been faithful to their trusts."[9]

As part of that trust, two prominent Democrats, Bankhead and Rountree, organized the North Alabama Good Roads Association. Like the Office of Public Roads at the federal level, it had as its basic purpose the diffusion of information concerning the construction and maintenance of roads. Just how interested the two Democratic Party leaders were in improving Alabama's public roads, however, remains in question. Certainly south Alabama had roads in equally as bad condition as those in the northern part of the state, and the argument can be made that the state's first active good roads organization came about more in response to disgruntled Democrats who had bolted from the party than as a result of the demands of grass-roots farmers. Thus, while the North Alabama Good Roads Association did begin because of Populism, it was not formed by impassioned left-wing farmers seeking relief from their miseries but by Democratic Party partisans who had little, if anything, other than votes to gain from road improvements.[10]

But whatever the motives of Bankhead and Rountree, both men retained their association with the North Alabama Good Roads Association for more than two decades. By 1898, Rountree had sold his interest in the Birmingham Age-Herald Publishing Company to start his own publishing firm and was, therefore, able to devote more time to the promotion of good roads than Congressman Bankhead, whose position of vice-president of the association required little work. For the decade following its inception, Rountree routinely oversaw membership in the North Alabama Good Roads Association, promoted a positive image of the organization through his connections with the Alabama Press Association, and organized whatever formal activities the association held each year. Good roads, among other popular New South causes, became a

theme for Rountree to regularly address in his two popular periodicals, *Dixie Home,* aimed at promoting "Progress in Manufacturing, Agriculture and Immigration," and *Dixie Manufacturer,*
which Rountree devoted to "Southern Industrial Progress." Both
were published from the Birmingham offices of the Rountree Publishing Company.[11]

By 1906, when the North Alabama and the South Alabama Good
Roads associations merged to form the Alabama Good Roads Association, Rountree had become a well-recognized and well-respected
leader in the campaign for good roads in his state. Both business
leaders and farmers paid him tribute, which was evident in 1907
when he addressed the Birmingham Motor Club to propose a
transstate highway from Tennessee south to Mobile. He suggested
that the route be intersected by local road systems in each county
through which it passed. Although at this early date there was no
talk of the tourist revenue the proposed highway would generate,
the Mobile Commercial Club "enthusiastically endorsed" the idea,
as did farmers' organizations in Cullman, Blount, Morgan, and
Winston counties, perceiving the proposed highway as a means
of improving farmers' ability to get their crops to market. The
Alabama Farmers' Union, as yet unaware of the turn toward highway construction that the good roads movement in the South would
soon take, even urged its ninety thousand members to work dili-
gently to make the highway a reality.[12]

Rountree's approach to the betterment of public roads in Alabama, however, was strictly business, and he always steered a careful
course away from political controversy. By calling attention to the
progress other states were making in the improvement of their roads
and by constantly citing the litany of benefits good roads would
bring, the Birmingham publisher may not have had as much success in actually getting roads improved as he did in selling himself
as a hardworking, civic-minded, responsible businessman who saw
an opportunity to better his state and his region. Many local
newspapers throughout Alabama responded by printing their approval of his efforts. The *North Alabamian* of Tuscumbia praised
him for educating the public on the subject of good roads, and

Members of the Alabama Good Roads Association, which was formed in 1906, took a break from their promotion of road improvements to enjoy a slice of watermelon, ca. 1911. Sporting a mustache and a hat, John Asa Rountree stands in the second row, fourth from the right. Courtesy of the Birmingham Public Library, Archives Division.

the Midland City *Enterprise* recognized the *Dixie Manufacturer* "as the organ of the Good Roads Movement through the South." But perhaps more importantly, Rountree succeeded in convincing Alabama business leaders, who regularly read his publications, that better roads were essential to economic development, and as much a part of a New South as education and commerce. To advance this notion further, Rountree convinced the Birmingham business community in 1910 to publicize the progress that Alabama had made in the improvement of its roads by inviting the National Good Roads Association to hold its fourth annual convention in Birmingham the following year.[13]

By 1913, as we saw in chapter one, hundreds of good roads associations had sprung up throughout the country. But contrary to its name, the National Good Roads Association – unlike the older National League for Good Roads, organized in 1892, and the American Automobile Association's American Road Congress – represented the interests of only a small number of Americans. It was conceived in Chicago in 1907 by Arthur C. Jackson, who presided over it and three other such associations: the International Good Roads and Automobile Association, the Illinois State Good Roads Association, and the Chicago Good Roads Association.

Jackson appointed Rountree secretary of the 1911 meeting, and together they managed to attract 1,422 delegates from seventeen states and the District of Columbia to Birmingham on 23 and 24 May. These delegates adopted several resolutions calling on Congress to create a national bureau of public roads and empower it to administer a federally subsidized national roads program.[14] But as good roads meetings went, the 1911 National Good Roads Association convention was nothing out of the ordinary, except that it introduced Rountree to the possibility of going national with his own good roads campaign.

For several years the Birmingham publisher had visualized a more far-reaching good roads organization. The Alabama Good Roads Association had become less than satisfactory to him, and in March 1908, when only six members attended a regularly sched-

uled meeting, he wrote to the Association's vice-president and
newly elected United States senator, John Hollis Bankhead, that
a permanent organization would be a good idea politically. "We
want to elect the next legislature of Alabama on a platform committed to create a highway commission" and, he added parenthe-
tically, "to take care of our friends." Rountree failed to get very
far with this idea, but at the 1911 meeting in Birmingham, he and
Jackson formed a committee to look into the possibility of organizing existing good roads associations throughout the nation into one
unified body. Rountree and Jackson worked on this concept for
almost two years and in March 1913 managed to convince Birmingham business leaders to give the new umbrella association a
name – the National Good Roads Federation – and to proceed with
plans for a formal organizational meeting in Birmingham on 24
and 25 April.[15] One thing, however, was missing: the blessing of
John Hollis Bankhead, who, by 1913, had distinguished himself
as a national leader of the campaign for good roads. Without his
endorsement, the success of the new National Good Roads Federation, Rountree realized, was in serious doubt.

Because of what had happened between Bankhead and Rountree at the end of 1912, the senator showed little enthusiasm for
either the Birmingham publisher or his ambitious scheme. In
December 1912, Bankhead had learned that Rountree had been
using his name to solicit membership in the Alabama Good Roads
Association, telling prospective members that the senator had recommended them. Bankhead wrote Rountree that he could "not recall
having suggested anyone's name in this connection" and let his good
roads associate know in no uncertain terms that he was to refrain
from any such practice in the future.

Bankhead's displeasure with him, however, failed to dissuade
Rountree from including the senator in his plans for the National
Good Roads Federation. On 1 March 1913, Rountree wrote Bankhead, asking him to preside over the federation's organizational
meeting and agree to serve as its first president. On the same day,
Rountree sent a letter to C. B. Beasley, an acquaintance of Bankhead's living in Washington, requesting assistance in gaining the

senator's acceptance. The following Tuesday, 4 March, Rountree was to meet with representatives of the Birmingham Chamber of Commerce, Business Men's League, Board of Trade, and the Jefferson County Good Roads Association to finalize plans for the proposed organizational convention, and he wanted Beasley to make sure that Bankhead had telegraphed his acceptance in time for the meeting.[16]

Rountree did receive a telegram from Bankhead regarding the proposed convention, but in it the senator declined the invitation. A few days later, Bankhead's private secretary wrote Rountree confirming the nonacceptance and advised him that the senator would make his reasons for not wanting to participate in the convention known the next time he was in Birmingham. Rountree, however, refused to take "no" for an answer. On 18 March, the same date two officials of the Birmingham Chamber of Commerce wrote Bankhead urging him to "be present and address this noble gathering," Rountree sent another invitation to Bankhead in Washington, this time on official stationery with the letterhead, "National Good Roads Federation, J. A. Rountree, Secretary-in-Charge." Rountree said he was writing at the instruction of the executive committee of the federation and prodded the senator with unmistakable progressive reasoning. "The object of the Federation," he advised, "is to organize the advocates of Improved Highways in one grand consolidated body; to aid in securing Federal, State and County aid for the building of Improved Highways; to conduct an educational campaign and to awake activity in Highway Improvement."[17]

On the same day, 18 March, Rountree wrote Bankhead a second letter, this time enclosing a press clipping from the Birmingham *Age-Herald* announcing the April meeting. In this second letter, Rountree informed the senator that he foresaw the federation meeting as being bigger and better than either the 1911 National Good Roads Congress or one the Office of Public Roads had held in 1912 in Atlantic City, New Jersey. "Now I am depending upon you calling this convention to order, delivering an address, and presiding over the same. You are the man," he pointed out, "who started this idea . . . and it is nothing but proper and right that you shall preside over this meeting."[18]

Over the next ten days Rountree kept the pressure on. He had several Birmingham business and political leaders contact Bankhead and urge him to accept the invitation. On 26 March, the senator returned to Birmingham, where he met with Rountree, about the matter. The next day the *Age-Herald* carried a story indicating that Bankhead had completely changed his mind and was "quite enthusiastic" about the convention and his role in it. The newspaper reported that Bankhead was in complete approval of the newly formed National Good Roads Federation objectives. Earlier in his congressional career, the story continued, Bankhead had advocated the consolidation of many rivers and harbors associations into one organization and, it stated, he "desires to see the same kind of body for the good roads people of this country."[19]

In truth, Bankhead had serious reservations about accepting the presidency of the National Good Roads Federation, and as he revealed later, "doubted the wisdom of attempting an organization as broad in its character." But whatever misgivings the senator may have had, Rountree managed to keep them hidden. And after the press publicly committed him to the goal of the federation, Bankhead quickly found himself in a position of having to defend the very motives of the federation's organizer that he had earlier questioned.

Rountree realized that if the United States Office of Public Roads sent a road building model and one of its field representatives to Birmingham for the April meeting, the federation would be given added legitimacy. When he encountered stiff resistance to a request for this model from Logan Waller Page, director of the federal agency, Rountree asked Bankhead to discuss the matter with Page's boss, Secretary of Agriculture David F. Houston. In his letter to Houston, Bankhead noted Page's antipathy for private good roads organizations but, since the desired road building model was only in nearby Montgomery, he questioned why Page had so adamantly refused to allow it to be sent to the Birmingham meeting.[20]

Two days later, on 17 April, Bankhead received a confidential letter from Secretary Houston, who had discussed the matter with Page. Page had informed the secretary that Rountree was "totally ignorant of the road situation" and was holding the convention solely for personal profit. Houston considered Rountree's alliance with Arthur Jackson anything but reputable because Jackson, as he put it, was already involved in similar "nefarious schemes for making money," and the Department of Agriculture was in the process of having him investigated. "I consider it to be unwise," Houston allowed, "to have anything to do with an association with which he [Jackson] is connected." Houston went on to apprise the senator of the department's policy of cooperation with all existing good roads associations in the country, with the exception of those with which Jackson had any relationship. Houston further informed Senator Bankhead that the last time Page had been in Birmingham, Rountree had treated him "in the most humiliating manner."[21]

Bankhead responded to Houston's letter on the day he received it. Whether Houston had confirmed what Bankhead already knew or suspected about Rountree was not evident in the senator's reply. Instead, he came to Rountree's defense. He stated that he could say "without contradiction" that Rountree had "never received a dollar" from his good roads work and that, as far as he knew, the Birmingham publisher had absolutely no connection with the shadowy Jackson, whom he called a "fakir." "I would be very glad to see [Jackson] put out of business," he stated conclusively. "I have known for some time that he was being investigated [for postal fraud]."[22]

Bankhead became acquainted with Jackson in 1911 when they both attended the National Good Roads Association convention in Birmingham, but the senator apparently had no knowledge of Jackson's role in the formation of the new National Good Roads Federation. This, however, was enough to raise the aging senator's interest in the Birmingham meeting. And on the evening of 23 April, when he stepped off the train from Washington in the Birmingham station, Bankhead made his feelings about the matter emphatically known to Rountree. Thereafter, Jackson's name was never mentioned again in connection with the federation, and to make sure that Jackson's National Good Roads Association had absolutely no connection with the new National Good Roads Federation, Rountree changed the name of his organization. As of 24 April 1913, it became the United States Good Roads Association.

New name or old, the United States Good Roads Association, the first and only national good roads association ever headquartered in the South, got off to a shaky start. One of the individuals most closely connected with its conception was being threatened with a federal investigation; the proposed president of the new organization had grave misgivings about the whole idea of another national good roads association; and fewer than nine hundred of the several thousand delegates its major proponent, J. Asa Rountree, publicly announced would attend the USGRA organizational meeting actually showed up. Nevertheless, the convention went on as scheduled.

Rountree hired an orchestra to serenade his guests and had Birmingham's Jefferson Theatre, site of the convention, decorated with festive banners. When Senator Bankhead arrived in town, he made it clear that he would make no speeches nor publicly endorse the USGRA in any way. Bankhead's presence, however, accomplished enough. Even though the senator departed Birmingham before the convention adjourned, he had associated himself with Rountree's cause. In the short time he was at the convention, Rountree saw to it that the delegates elected the senator permanent president of the USGRA, and as a token of his appreciation, Rountree and several other convention members presented Bankhead with an ebony, gold-headed cane inscribed, "Presented to John Hollis Bankhead, First President of the United States Good Roads Association." The convention adopted a number of resolutions that called for the usual federal aid to road building as well as the establishment of a five-member committee to call on President Woodrow Wilson regarding good roads legislation. Convention delegates also approved a plan to hold a second meeting in November 1913 in St. Louis and appointed St. Louis businessman and promoter Thomas L. Cannon, who was the secretary-manager of the St. Louis Convention Bureau, as the association's managing director.[23]

Apparently, Rountree was swayed by Cannon's optimistic claim that he could attract between fifteen and twenty-five thousand dues-paying delegates to St. Louis, as well as road-building equipment manufacturers, concrete contractors, and other roads-related exhibitors who would pay to advertise their goods and services before such a large gathering. Cannon also agreed to provide front money to promote the November meeting and to share all profits on a fifty-fifty basis. Within a matter of weeks after Rountree had approved this plan, however, he realized not only that Cannon could not deliver the funds he had promised to promote the meeting but that control of the United States Good Roads Association was slip-

The founding members of the United States Good Roads Association assembled on the steps of the Jefferson Theater in Birmingham, Alabama, in April 1913. Senator John Hollis Bankhead, Sr. (heaviest man standing in front row) is flanked by John Asa Rountree to his left and Colonel Thomas S. Plowden, who later served as president of the Bankhead National Highway Association, to his right. Courtesy of the Birmingham Public Library, Archives Division.

ping from his grasp. "I had my doubts about the Exposition at St. Louis being a success," he wrote Bankhead retrospectively on 24 May. "[I cannot afford] to work for nothing," he said, "and also pay expenses." Rountree feared that, if the convention failed, he would be blamed and the USGRA would be dead. "If something is not done to work up the convention and make it a success," he informed Bankhead on 20 August, "the meeting will be a frost [and] you and I will get the cussing."[24]

Bankhead acknowledged Rountree's disappointment and confessed that the situation was not very encouraging. At the same time, he wrote to Cannon in St. Louis that he had neither the time nor the inclination to raise money for the meeting and that, if Cannon remembered correctly, he had "most earnestly protested against accepting the Presidency of [the] Association" in the first place. Nevertheless, he wanted the St. Louis meeting to be successful and asked Cannon to write him about the matter as soon as possible. Bankhead did not hear from Cannon immediately and, in the meantime, received another letter from Rountree in Birmingham complaining bitterly that Cannon was planning on selling memberships in the United States Good Roads Association to pay for the needed promotional expenses. As far as Rountree was concerned, this was the last straw. Cannon was encroaching on a source of profit from which he intended to operate the association and to pay himself. He called Cannon an "optimistic blower" who had not accomplished anything and told Bankhead that he had already advised the directors of the organization that the best thing to do was call off the St. Louis meeting altogether.[25]

Bankhead, on the other hand, was unwilling to cancel the meeting. As he told his Birmingham colleague on 10 September, he had extended invitations to the governors of the forty-eight states, who had already appointed delegates. "It would be a serious matter now," he cautioned, "to take the action indicated in your [4 September] letter." Bankhead made it clear that Rountree should not expect to profit in any way from the November meeting and, without warning, suggested to Rountree that "if I were you, I would resign the position of Secretary and state as a reason that the press of business makes it impossible for you to give the matter prompt attention." He also informed Rountree that, at the next meeting of the USGRA, he intended to resign the position of president "and under no circumstances would . . . again accept an official connection with the Association."

Rountree was shaken. Immediately after he read what the senator had in mind, he fired off a six-page letter explaining his position. He said he regretted Bankhead's plan to resign as president and, in a matter-of-fact yet flattering statement, said that he thought the decision would be fatal to the organization. "No one regrets more than I do," he lamented, "that the Association seems doomed to be a failure," but as to his own resignation, he explained that he preferred to step down when Bankhead did and to give his own reasons for doing so.[26]

Less than a week after Rountree mailed his lengthy letter to Washington, Bankhead returned home to Jasper, Alabama, for a brief vacation. On 19 October, Rountree traveled the forty miles between Birmingham and Jasper to confer with Bankhead and, in the quiet of the senator's home, managed to smooth over past difficulties. They agreed to let Cannon handle the convention entirely from St. Louis and, as Rountree wrote Bankhead a day later, allow St. Louis to "make a success or failure of it." In Jasper, Rountree successfully downed any negative feelings that the crusty old senator may have had toward him and, by appealing to Bankhead's vanity, returned to Birmingham with both his long-cultivated relationship with Bankhead and his position as secretary of the USGRA still intact. Rountree's salesmanship was evident the next time Bankhead corresponded with Cannon.

> I believe the best thing you can do is to ignore any reflections upon Rountree. [He] is my devoted friend and I am not willing to wound his feelings unnecessarily. I have suggested to him the propriety of resigning as there were no available funds to pay him for his work. This was sometime ago, but he does not seem to take kindly to the suggestion and I have, therefore, dropped the matter.

The one problem, however, that Rountree was unable to overcome was Bankhead's strong desire to sever his relationship with the

USGRA. Rountree skillfully handled this by simply ignoring the senator's insistence, and although Bankhead made it clear publicly that he had resigned, Rountree continued to refer to him as president of the United States Good Roads Association.[27]

If Rountree learned anything in the five and a half months between the Birmingham and St. Louis meetings, it was that he could not entrust the success of the United States Good Roads Association to anyone but himself. Before the St. Louis convention, therefore, he persuaded the association's board of directors to oust Cannon, leaving him in control, a position he enjoyed from 1913 until his death in 1936. During each of these twenty-three years, as he had done in Birmingham in 1913, Rountree single-handedly organized a good roads convention. With a few exceptions, each annual meeting of the USGRA was held in a different southern or southwestern city. Rountree traveled to each convention site months in advance, established a headquarters in a prominent hotel, and sent out press releases announcing the names of ranking political and governmental leaders who, he stated publicly, would attend the meeting. He also met constantly with municipal officials and worked tirelessly to persuade local business leaders that a good roads convention in their city would attract thousands of visitors who would spend thousands of dollars. If he was able to sell this idea, chambers of commerce sometimes provided an auditorium or convention center for the meeting, and the local business community almost always helped defray the expense of organizing the event. As a result of his promotion, the numerous exhibitors he attracted, and the number of good roads advocates who paid to attend the meetings, Rountree did well financially.

Judging from the time Rountree spent each year organizing the USGRA convention and promoting its membership, by 1916 a substantial part of his livelihood must have come from these activities. Rountree solicited members by writing to prospective individuals and groups, stating that they had been recommended by a prominent business leader or public official already associated with the USGRA. He never employed a staff to do this work and was very careful never to reveal membership statistics. For one hundred dollars a person could become a sustaining member of the USGRA, for twenty-five dollars a life member, and for five dollars an annual member. Annual dues were one dollar.

Beginning in 1916, each member received a copy of the *United States Good Roads Bulletin,* which Rountree published monthly in Birmingham. The *Bulletin* was an advertisement both for good roads and for the New South. In its first issue and on the same page that he announced his twenty-one "Good Roads Maxims," Rountree included an article urging those outside the South to investigate the advantages and attractions of the region; he suggested in another passage that real estate in Alabama was a good investment; and in a third article, he quoted Henry Grady on the emergence of the New South.[28] In this and later editions of the *United States Good Roads Bulletin,* Rountree attempted to sell his readers on the idea that good roads and the New South were inseparable, but the kind of roads he had as a priority were definitely not farm-to-market roads.

In 1916, he came up with the scheme for a four-thousand-mile transcontinental tourist highway which he named in honor of Bankhead. The John Hollis Bankhead National Highway stretched from the District of Columbia, across the Deep South, through Texas, New Mexico, and Arizona, all the way to San Diego, California. Rountree made the trek from Washington to San Diego three separate times during the early 1920s soliciting support from men and women along the way who lived in communities through which the route of the highway passed. His message to them was as familiar as it was direct: support the Bankhead Highway Association and the United States Good Roads Association with your donations and membership, attend their annual conventions, and encourage other southerners to do the same, and your town will be immeasurably enriched by automobile tourist revenue. The success of the New South, in other words, could be measured directly by the success of Rountree's two good roads associations.

Rountree gave this notion credibility by securing the endorsement of influential state and federal government officials. In 1916,

An official of the Dallas, Texas, contingent of the Bankhead National Highway Association greets John Asa Rountree on the proposed Bankhead National Highway just east of Dallas, ca. 1920. Rountree made the transcontinental trek on the 4,000-mile interstate highway, which ran from Washington, D.C., to San Diego, three times during the early 1920s. Courtesy of the Birmingham Public Library, Archives Division.

he claimed that fourteen of the twenty-five members of the House Committee on Good Roads were members of the USGRA, as were twenty-eight of the nation's governors. The one public official who provided Rountree's work with its greatest credibility, however, was Bankhead, and Rountree constantly struggled – even naming a highway in the senator's honor – to prevent his estranged associate from severing his relationship with him and the USGRA altogether. Bankhead never got over his initial feeling of suspicion regarding the USGRA, but after he had publicly announced his resignation as president in 1913, he allowed Rountree to persuade him to recon-sider. Bankhead attempted to resign on at least two other occasions, once in 1914 and again in 1915, but each time, Rountree was able to appeal successfully to the senator's vanity and convince him to remain as president. In the summer of 1916, Rountree proclaimed Bankhead to be the "Father of the Federal Aid Road Act." With a title like that, with a national highway named after him, and with Rountree serv-ing as the highway association's director, Bankhead thereafter found it impossible to turn his back on either the USGRA or the Bankhead Highway Association. Consequently, up until 1 March 1920, the day of his death, John Hollis Bankhead, Sr., remained, if in name only, the first and only president of the United States Good Roads Associa-tion, and for the sake of public appearance, the close personal friend and valued mentor of John Asa Rountree.[29]

Rountree was a few days away from his fifty-third birthday when Senator Bankhead died. For the majority of his life, Rountree had been a promoter of causes. As a young newspaper editor in rural Alabama during the politically unsettled 1880s, Asa Rountree had seen the plight of farmers isolated from markets and the outside world by impassable road conditions. He responded by echoing their concerns and by seeking government assistance with road im-provements. But Rountree was no Populist. While his rural roots may have made him abundantly aware of the value of good roads, his wholehearted acceptance of New South ideology allowed him to substitute status, urban prominence, and, above all, profit for whatever populist notions he once entertained. When the automobile gave new meaning to the good roads movement in the South and highway progressives emerged to speak on behalf of road im-provements, priorities—as we have seen—changed. Because of their all-important drive to achieve a measure of prosperity equivalent to that in the North, and because there was no strong tradition of reform in the South, Rountree, for one, was able to take a na-tional progressive issue, turn it into a business venture, portray himself as a hardworking, forward-looking citizen, and profit finan-cially from his efforts. While other southerners discovered opportunities in banking, publishing, or commerce, Rountree found his in the good roads movement. Perhaps John Asa Rountree appears over-eager, and even dishonest, in his enthusiasm for good roads. But when viewed in the context of his day and time, he was less an aberration than an embodiment of southern progressivism: a man, like others of his persuasion, who fit the mold of New South promoter much better than he did that of reformer.

PART TWO

Automobility and Modernization

The Road South: 1910

The good roads movement failed to bring about the new rural South of less austerity and greater accessibility that farmers and progressive-thinking southerners originally projected. On the other hand, the campaign to build tourist highways did prove instrumental to the emergence of a different South: one that conformed more closely to national rather than regional standards, and one with a future that promised prosperity not to farmers but to the business community. Southerners got a glimpse of this New South once the first motorists began to set aside their trepidation about driving long-distance over the region's notoriously inadequate roads. One of the first of these fearless early automobile tourists was a Connecticut Yankee who brought his entire family into the South by motorcar in the fall of 1910.

To his friends and neighbors in Litchfield, Connecticut, Seymour Cunningham must have appeared to be either a hopeless eccentric or an utter fool. Cunningham was a prominent New Englander and a man of more than modest means, and the trip that he embarked on in 1910 took him, his wife, and four-year-old daughter more than a thousand miles from home and over hundreds of miles of the treacherous, often impassable, and largely unmapped roads of the South. Because it was less accessible to northern motorists in 1910 than it had been to the Union cavalry during the Civil War – a condition highway progressives would soon try to change – the American South was definitely not the best place to take a family on a motor outing. Cunningham, in fact, could not have picked an automobile excursion that offered more hazards. Traveling into the South by motorcar meant riding for days over bone-jarring rutted roads, fording streams and rivers, removing fallen trees and broken branches from roadways, getting stuck axle-deep in mud and sand, and possibly even being stranded for days in some remote wilderness by mechanical difficulty. In 1910, if anything was certain about long-distance automobile travel below the Mason-Dixon line, it was uncertainty.[1]

Long before the Cunninghams started on their adventure, roads in the South had a bad reputation. During the late nineteenth century, members of the League of American Wheelmen, an organization of bicyclists, bravely toured the Shenandoah Valley and parts of northern Virginia and had nothing but criticism for the road conditions. The most frequently traveled roads in the South at the turn of the century were built decades earlier by private citizens who charged a toll for their use. These toll roads were generally poorly maintained, and because most people who traveled them were on horseback, the owners had no reason to bridge the small streams and creeks the roads crossed. Consequently, as one motorist who risked a trip into Virginia in 1907 found out, "the ford [was] a permanent institution."[2] As late as 1910, when the Cunninghams set out on their trip, driving a motor vehicle into the South was very rare and was undertaken only by the most serious and experienced motorists.

Because the roads were so bad, and because of the limited availability of automobiles, northerners who came south regularly at the turn of the century were mostly health-seekers and wealthy vacationers who traveled by train or ocean steamer and who could afford the expense of staying at a resort. At that time, wintering in the South was very popular, and there was enough tourist trade to sustain large hotels like the Moorish Tampa Bay Hotel in Tampa, Florida, the rambling New Hampton Terrace Hotel at Thomasville, Georgia, and the luxurious Princess Anne Hotel in Virginia Beach, Virginia. Other popular spots spread along the railroad lines were

in Hot Springs and Asheville, North Carolina, in Aiken and Cam-
den, South Carolina, and on the east coast of Florida, where Henry
M. Flagler had opened colossal hotels at St. Augustine, Ormond
Beach, and Palm Beach.[3]

Then, beginning in 1902, Florida's east coast began to attract
the attention of Americans who liked to come south during the
winter months for a different reason. Automobile racing was becoming a popular pastime among the leisure class, and Ormond and
Daytona beaches were perfect for the sport. The mild winter climate
and broad, firm beaches attracted hundreds of visitors each winter
who came to the Sunshine State to watch daredevils like Glenn
Curtiss, Barney Oldfield, Vincenzo Lancia, and Louis Chevrolet
drive their fledgling machines down the beach at unheard-of
speeds. In addition, Savannah, Georgia, began to host similar
motorcar races and, by 1910, enjoyed the reputation of being a favorite racing center among members of the American Automobile
Club, which had its headquarters in New York City.[4]

Northerners who came to Florida in the winter to witness new
land speed records or simply to enjoy the sunshine often brought
their own motor vehicles with them, and at the conclusion of the
events each January, they began to seriously consider the possibility
of driving back north rather than returning by rail or steamer. Dar-
ing automobilists who risked their lives traveling cross-country were
receiving a great deal of publicity and praise from the growing number of automobile owners in the country. So by 1910, many less experienced motorists, influenced by the homage paid these drivers, were
simply willing to ignore better judgment and venture forth on the
treacherous roads that connected the North and the South.[5]

Despite its undeniable risks, motoring through the South held
great appeal to many Americans who contemplated long-distance
excursions by automobile. As early as 1907, the scenery of the
Shenandoah Valley and the history of the Civil War battlefields
in northern Virginia attracted a few automobile tourists. A report
of one such trip, whose author began by attempting to dispel the
then widespread rumor that Virginia was a roadless state, pictured
the arcadian wilderness and scenic adventure travelers could ex-

pect to experience.[6] In 1910 more automobile owners lived in the Northeast than in any other section of the country. By heading south, they felt they could test their driving skills under the most trying circumstances and without having to undertake a transcontinental trek. Many northerners already considered the South a convenient place to escape the rigors of urban-industrial life and, at the same time, enjoy a milder winter climate. And while the roads were horrendous, greater distances between towns and cities in the South than in the more densely populated Northeast offered motorists the challenge they wanted. Perhaps one writer best expressed the view of many automobilists in 1910 when he wrote that the South was "a country of magnificent distances with sparse population as compared to the North."[7]

During the first decade of the twentieth century, there was also a desire among some travelers to "See America First." Americans of this persuasion were willing to forego the comforts and refinements of European travel for an opportunity to explore their own country. Seymour Cuningham felt this urge deeply. He had traveled abroad, was a member of both the infant American Automobile Association (AAA) and the Litchfield Automobile Club, and had made several weekend jaunts between New England towns. But, when it came to long-distance travel in a motorcar, Cunningham was a neophyte. Never had he motored so far from home that, in the event of mechanical difficulty, help was unavailable. He placed great faith in his touring car, a sturdy Pierce-Arrow 48, and aspired to the kind of touring he had read about in the *American Motorist*, a monthly publication of the AAA. He was captivated by reports of transcontinental automobile reliability runs made by twentieth-century motoring heroes like fellow New Englander H. Nelson Jackson, who seven years earlier had driven from San Francisco all the way to New York City in a matter of only sixty-three days. If Jackson could do it, why couldn't he? After all, he was planning on going only as far as Charleston, South Carolina.[8]

Prior to 1910, the AAA received hundreds of requests for routing information into the southern United States. But not until then

When this small Durham County, North Carolina, section of the National Highway—which stretched from New York City to Atlanta—was paved, most of the back-breaking work was done by hand, including building the form for the concrete, ca. 1919. This route, the one the AAA first recommended in 1910 as the most reliable leading south, was the one the Cunninghams followed as far as Charlotte.

did the organization include a section mapping a portion of the South in its annual publication, *The Automobile Blue Book*. Although this map was scant in detail and by no means a complete travel guide, a brief accompanying article provided some encouragement. "It is probable that there will be a great increase of travel to and from the south within the next year," the AAA stated, "and it is the expectation of the Blue Book to materially extend its work in the states through which these routes will run." Following publication of the *1910 Blue Book*, the *American Motorist* carried a two-part article entitled "Touring to Dixie." Its author, Robert Bruce, described the growing urge of American motorists to drive into the South during the coming winter, but he was careful to remind his readers that it would be at least three years before the AAA could compile, organize, and publish a detailed routing guide for the region. The two articles, however, were very positive and gave no indication that a trip by automobile between the North and South would be unsafe.[9]

Bruce found the National Highway leading south from Hagerstown, Maryland, through the Shenandoah Valley to Roanoke, across the Piedmont to Winston-Salem and Charlotte, and then on to Atlanta to be the most popular; but he added that he believed the growing commercial interests in eastern and central Virginia, the Carolinas, Georgia, and Florida would soon draw travelers to other parts of the South. Bruce also provided his readers with the most current mileage figures between stops along the National Highway and recommended volume three of the *1910 Blue Book* as the only reliable touring guide with complete enough route information between Hagerstown and Atlanta.[10] At that early date there were no markers pointing directions through a town or indicating which fork on a remote rural road a driver must take to stay on course. Routing information, even if it lacked detail, was an absolute necessity, and Bruce was quick to point out that, while the *1910 Blue Book* was sketchy in places, it was nonetheless reliable.

The *1910 Blue Book*, the first automobile guide between North and South, was the culmination of two years of "route making" below the Mason-Dixon line by R. H. "Pathfinder" Johnston. On two separate occasions during 1908, Johnston blazed trails for motorists through the South. His first trek took twenty-five days, beginning in Philadelphia on 12 January and ending in Savannah, Georgia, on 7 February. This unprecedented journey took him through Gettysburg; the District of Columbia; Wheeling, West Virginia; Columbus and Cincinnati, Ohio; Lexington and Louisville, Kentucky; Nashville, Tennessee; Huntsville, Alabama; Chattanooga; Atlanta; and finally to Savannah. Much of this distance was unmapped, and Johnston had to rely upon information he gleaned from Civil War records to determine the correct routes between towns and cities. South of Nashville the roads were particularly bad, but so was the directional advice. Johnston claimed to have asked some two hundred people how to get to Chattanooga, and before he finally rolled into town, he came to the conclusion that the Tennessee city located in the shadow of Lookout Mountain was a place nature had attempted to hide from the rest of the world. Upon completion of the trip, however, Johnston unhesitatingly recommended the excursion to "all tourists who have good sturdy touring cars."

Johnston had good reason to promote the route he had opened rather than warn prospective tourists of the trip's impending dangers. He realized that potentially great commercial opportunities existed for the sale of a guidebook that traced every turn in the road. At that time, Johnston was the advertising director for the White Motorcar Company of Cleveland, Ohio, and this, his first motor trip into the South, was as much a commercial venture as a pathfinding adventure. His route was made into a running guide, given the title of *White Route, Book Number Six,* and was successfully marketed by the White Motorcar Company. (See map 5.)

Later that year, however, Johnston realized an even greater opportunity. With the racing events in Savannah becoming more and more popular each year, he reasoned that

> many tourists are now considering the possbility of either traveling southward to the [Georgia] course by motor car, or of touring northward at their leisure after the race [concludes]. Furthermore, the season of the year is approaching when thousands of residents of the North invade the southland to escape the rigors of the northern winter.

His thinking brought him to the conclusion that there would soon be even more demand for another more eastern automobile route between the North and South. He blazed his second trail in the fall of 1908, but unlike the other route, this one started in the South and ended in the North. Johnston began in Savannah and from there went to Atlanta; Anderson and Spartanburg, South Carolina; Charlotte and Winston-Salem, North Carolina; Roanoke and Staunton, Virginia; Hagerstown, Maryland; Philadelphia; and New York City. (See map 5.)

Map 5. First automobile routes linking North and South, 1908.

He made this trip much more quickly than the first, taking careful notes to define the route as clearly and closely as possible. Before he published his second touring guide, Johnston made a critical observation of the year he had spent traveling by automobile through the South. "The joys—or the sorrows—of touring in the South," he wrote, "depend entirely on the weather man. If it rains, the roads no longer merit the name, and one wonders if the phrase 'The Sunny South,' is a delusion."[11]

This second trip by Johnston set the stage for the widely publicized automobile adventure below the Mason-Dixon line, jointly sponsored by the Atlanta *Journal* and the New York *Herald*, that piqued the enthusiasm of Leonard Tufts. The reliability run covered much of the same route that Johnston had charted the previous fall, but unlike other contests of its day, the New York to Atlanta marathon attracted manufacturers who wished to advertise the durability of their vehicles. And because so many of the contestants who started the race actually finished, motoring safely into the South gained greater credibility.

This event, which saw thirty-eight contestants' cars and nine officials' cars leave Broadway on 25 October 1909 and thirteen days later arrive on Peachtree Street in downtown Atlanta, also provided an occasion for southerners to promote the need for better roads. To stimulate local road improvement campaigns, the two sponsoring newspapers offered a prize of one thousand dollars to the county along the route that had the best stretch of roadway. But more importantly, the 1909 New York to Atlanta reliability run made possible the publication of volume three of the *Blue Book* and caused one source to go so far as to proclaim that the new southern route "removed all doubt as to the practicality of motor trips that way, and made the South a touring fixture."[12]

Encouraging words like these, which appeared in the *Journal* and the *Herald*, as well as the coverage the reliability contest received in popular motoring periodicals like the *American Motorist, Automobile,* and *The Club Journal* generated a great deal of interest in making the trip south via motor vehicle in 1910. As late as the autumn of that year, volume three of the *Blue Book* remained the most widely available and reliable source of information a motorist could have when driving into the South. When Seymour Cunningham contemplated his own trip to Charleston, South Carolina, in 1910, the first thing he did was obtain a copy of the *Blue Book*.

Cunningham and his family departed Litchfield on 16 November 1910 laden with enough equipment and supplies to confront almost any emergency. He had read the list of gear the AAA recommended for long-distance automobile tours and for months had tried to prepare for the unpredictable mishaps which he would inevitably face. The extent of his preparations was a credit to Cunningham's thoughtful planning, but it was also an affirmation of how inaccessible the South was to most Americans in 1910.

His most important consideration was to avoid getting stuck in the mud and stranded on some out-of-the-way road miles from the nearest town. As a precaution, Cunningham packed sets of tire chains and mud hooks, an axe, an electric flashlight, a shovel, a crowbar, one hundred feet of strong Manila rope, cement, and an ample supply of soapstone. In case mechanical difficulty developed, he carried some small valve parts, extra brake linings, five gallons of motor oil, a large bucket of grease, tire tubes and patches, a full set of brake shoes, and all the tools he had found indispensable on previous short outings. For personal comfort, the family wore heavy clothing and carried raincoats, galoshes, and an extra pair of shoes. They also took along an oilskin canvas large enough to cover the entire car and serve as a tarpaulin in the event of inclement weather. Mrs. Cunningham filled a large lunch basket with a variety of canned goods, and on the back of the Pierce-Arrow they strapped a trunk containing a change of clothing for the entire family. And finally, like generations of American explorers before him who had braved the uncertainties of each new frontier, Cunningham packed two absolute essentials, a compass and a gun. "Although all these things were not needed," he later wrote, "I should take every one of them again if repeating the trip."[13]

The Cunninghams proceeded south in "easy stages." For the first five days they drove through Connecticut, New York, Pennsylvania, and West Virginia on roads Cunningham described as generally very good. Then on 21 November, they entered northern Virginia with its panorama of mountains and stopped for the night in the Shenandoah Valley at Middletown. The following day they took a side trip to the mysterious Luray Caverns. Cunningham thoroughly enjoyed his walk through the caverns but found the deviation from the recommended route rough on his car and, before returning to the main road, he wired for an extra brake shoe and a few spare inner tubes.

Back on the established route, the party made Lexington, Virginia, with little difficulty. They spent the next day inspecting the highly publicized Natural Bridge, and like a real America Firster, Cunningham pronounced it "truly one of the natural wonders of the world." The road south to Roanoke was poor, but nothing compared to the next thirty-nine miles over the mountains between Roanoke and Rocky Mount. Cunningham described the road as the "worst imaginable," with very severe grades, treacherous fords, bad surfaces, and hairpin turns. The remaining miles through Virginia were equally testing, but once the party crossed into North Carolina, they found the going better. In Winston-Salem they registered at the old Zinzendorf Hotel and, for the next several days, relaxed, visiting the famous Moravian Cemetery near Salem College and enjoying the company of tobacco magnate R. J. Reynolds, who gave them a personal tour through one of his large factories.

On 29 November the Cunninghams left Winston-Salem and, with little difficulty, covered the eighty miles to Charlotte before nightfall. They remained there for several days, awaiting better weather before undertaking the last and most difficult phase of their journey. The *Blue Book* gave directions from Charlotte via Spartanburg, Greenville, and Anderson, South Carolina, to Atlanta. But the route from Charlotte to Charleston was totally uncharted, and like R. H. Johnston, Cunningham had to rely entirely upon individuals along the way for directional advice. He managed to obtain a primitive map from a Charlotte garage which specified the route as far as Camden, South Carolina. But the map did not give the mileage between towns and in no way prepared them for what lay ahead. Just south of Charlotte, the macadam paving ended, and from there on Cunningham described the driving as "simply fearful, [with] nothing but mud [which was] so soft and soapy" that the Pierce-Arrow crept along in first gear. It was on this leg of the trip that the mud hooks came in handy. While fording a shallow stream, the car became stuck. Cunningham jumped into the water, attached the mud hooks, and within a matter of minutes, had the travelers back on dry ground.

Their next stop was Camden, a popular resort for winter tourists. But Cunningham was displeased with the garage accommodations there and decided to push on to Columbia before dark. They stayed the night in the newly renovated Colonia, which a local newspaper said was "built to serve a tourist clientele of the best class." After breakfast the next morning, they crossed the Congaree River on the final segment of their trek and headed toward the coast. Heavy sand and badly rutted roads were their greatest problem until they left the Sandhills part of the state and neared Charleston. Swamps were the next inconvenience they encountered, and just before stopping for the night, they crossed two insect-infested quagmires named "Fourhole Swamp" and "Ten Bridges."[14]

After a short stay in the resort community of Summerville, the twenty-three-and-a-half-mile distance to Charleston proved uneventful, compared to the adventures of the previous weeks. They rolled into Charleston on the afternoon of 19 December, and the following day, the Charleston *News and Courier* reported their excursion as "one of the longest automobile trips on record."[15] This undoubtedly made Seymour Cunningham very proud. He had successfully completed a thirty-four-day trek, proving that he was no novice when it came to cross-country motor travel. He had forded streams and rivers in his motorcar and, without mishap, had negotiated some of the most treacherous roads imaginable in a region of the United States not known for its advancements, especially when it came to road building. While many weekend automobilists dreamed of undertaking such an ambitious adventure, Cunningham had actually lived it, and the article he wrote for the *American Motorist* the following March reflected his great satisfaction.

Regardless of his newfound sense of accomplishment, however, Cunningham's trip was not unprecedented. By 1910, cross-country jaunts in motor vehicles had become commonplace in America. Had he made the trip a few years earlier, in conjunction with an organized reliability run, or to publicize a particular make of motor vehicle, Cunningham might have received greater attention. His leisurely pace and his reluctance to venture too far from the established route proved that he was no trailblazer or pathfinder. Nevertheless, his trip did have significance. The way the Cunninghams traveled the eleven-hundred-mile distance between Litchfield and Charleston was both reminiscent of the way Americans traveled during the nineteenth century and, at the same time, suggestive of the way they would travel in years to come.

Because Cunningham had toured Europe by train, he had become accustomed to a style of travel that was both comfortable and predictable. His trip into the South in 1910 reflected this. Although he adhered to no specific timetable, Cunningham did maintain an itinerary and, like most nineteenth-century rail travelers, scheduled both his family's meals and overnight stays in hotels. His trip was less casual than it was structured, and while this style of travel remained the most popular, certain things about the Cunninghams' trip pointed to a new direction and understanding of travel in America.

Traveling by car allowed Cunningham a flexibility he had not known while touring abroad by train. He had made side trips to Luray Caverns and Natural Bridge, Virginia, and to the Moravian settlement in North Carolina. His pace was not hasty, perhaps because the roads were so bad, but also because he enjoyed the new freedom automobile travel afforded him. Escaping part of the harsh New England winter was also a part of Cunningham's motivation. "I had long been anxious to escape the rigors of a New England winter," he wrote the following year in the *American Motorist*.[16] In addition, the trip credited Cunningham with a certain rugged dignity which, by 1910, was popular in America. But his idea of pleasure was not camping out under the stars, cooking over an open fire, or facing the day-to-day problems that unmarked, unimproved roads offered. The automobile had yet to ring out that characteristic in Americans.

Cunningham was no pioneer, but his trip had a perspective of both the past and the future. It, and others like it, marked a watershed in the history of American motor travel. More durable cars, clearly marked routes, and up-to-date routing information enabled motorists to exchange a predictable, inflexible style of travel for one that offered more freedom and leisure. And the most important improvements bringing this change about were the construction and proper maintenance of roads, not only in the South but nationwide. Limited access by road, as well as by rail, had inhibited the South's growth both culturally and economically; and by the time Seymour Cunningham wheeled into Charleston, campaigns to improve local roads in the South, as we have seen, were well underway. Upon his arrival, Cunningham was probably unaware of the interest southerners had shown for decades in the condition of their roads and in the need to improve them. When he talked to the Charleston newspaper reporter, he did, however, make one recommendation: "If you will improve the bad places in your roads," he said, "automobilists in the hundreds will come from the North every spring."[17] With the passage of a few short years, and with the shift in emphasis of road improvement efforts from farm-to-market roads to interstate highways, Cunningham's observation indeed proved to be prophetic.

5

The Pneumatic Hegira

The formation of regional highway associations, like the Dixie Highway Association and the Lee Highway Association, promoting well-defined, clearly marked routes leading into the South from other parts of the nation opened the region for the first time to the outside world. These routes gave the South the accessibility it never before had. And more durable automobiles, in addition to more accurate and reliable routing guides, helped abate the concerns of many travel-conscious Americans who yearned to escape the sameness of everyday life and hit the open road.

Even with better maps and cars, however, touring over the notoriously bad roads of the South was undertaken with great caution and careful planning. Up until the end of the World War I, the region's reputation for unimproved, even dangerous, roads kept many American motorists away; but by the early 1920s, fear of traveling by car below the Mason-Dixon line disappeared, and tourists came south like never before. The destination of many of these first-time visitors was Florida, which emerged as a neo-frontier replete with all the necessary elements of past frontiers, including individualism, naturalism, and even heroism. The main difference between this twentieth-century frontier and earlier ones was that the central character was not the traditional frontiersman, the hardy yeoman farmer, or even the rugged trailblazer. The intrepid automobile tourist had taken their place.

What caused middle-class Americans to disregard their better judgment and motivated them to risk a trip over the South's treacherous roads was a popular understanding of the region that transcended the reality of its backwardness. This impressionistic view of the region had been cultivated for more than a half-century by nineteenth-century writers, artists, and illustrators whose aim was to depict the South from a romantic perspective. If the fanaticism and overblown simplicity that northern antebellum writers like James Russell Lowell, John Greenleaf Whittier, Wendell Phillips, and William Lloyd Garrison exhibited in their portrayal of the morally depraved Old South fanned the fires of extremism and ultimately contributed to a national myopia toward the region, this post–Civil War crop of writers who spread a romanticized version of the same geographical section may have advanced the region with equal, if not greater, misrepresentation. These writers possessed neither the moralistic convictions nor the same penchant for criticism that fired their predecessors. But while antebellum writers helped divide North and South, postbellum writers who chose the South as their subject and nurtured its romantic image unwittingly provided both northerners and southerners with a common ground of understanding, even if it was imaginary.

The manner in which late nineteenth-century writers portrayed the South was also a response to the rampant and disruptive forces of industrialism. Still overwhelmingly agrarian, and for the most part unscathed by industrialization, the South held great appeal to writers who sought to remind Americans that certain cherished virtues had not been altogether lost or abandoned. Hospitality, a slower pace of life, balmy winter weather, refined gentility, bucolic landscapes, and charm were all part of the image that writers and publishers perpetuated to appeal to citified Yankees who lived in colder climates.

At the turn of the century, this picture-postcard South, popularized in advertisements, landscape paintings, magazine articles, travel accounts, guidebooks, investment schemes, and woodcut illustrations, was the most visible impression Americans had of the region. By the time motorists began driving into the South, romanticism remained the standard upon which travel writers relied when describing places of interest. Much of the early twentieth-century travel literature about the region appearing in popular motoring magazines like the *American Motorist* and *Motor Travel* used romantic imagery to appeal to Americans interested in making an excursion into the South. As highway associations succeeded in promoting routes leading into the South, thereby raising Americans' expectations about the possibility of making a trip there in a motorcar, thousands upon thousands of tourists flooded the region, bringing the outside world with them. By 1930 the combination of interstate highways and automobility had greatly accelerated the pace of cultural conformity, so much so that some perceived this to be the end of the South.

As it had during the nineteenth century, the generally warmer, more inviting climate of the South made the region popular with early twentieth-century Americans, like Seymour Cunningham, who sought a refuge from harsher winter weather found elsewhere in the nation. Generally, early American motorists traveled from east to west during the spring and summer, but as the roads below the Mason-Dixon line improved, touring into the South during autumn and winter became popular. Where travel to Hudson Bay, the Yukon, the Sierra Nevada Mountains, or some other exotic vacation paradise was tantalizing to nature-loving automobile owners who dreamed of country life and itched to point their vehicles in the direction of a distant wilderness, these places, especially late in the year, were too far removed from the centers of civilization to be considered seriously by many motorists as vacation possibilities. Consequently, automobile owners residing in the North, who may have flinched at the thought of actually roughing it in the wild for a month or two, put the more proximate South atop their list of accessible wildernesses.

With an automobile, a family could vacation in the country, take advantage of all that nature had to offer, and in the South—as opposed to the Yukon or Hudson Bay—still maintain an important contact with civilization. These men and women, who raised "literary commuting" to new heights, formed the nucleus of the popular

turn-of-the-century back-to-nature and country life movements
which saw countless dissatisfied, restless Americans seek ways to
retreat from city life to a more serene arcadian environment.[1] The
prospect of a motoring excursion into the South, a region that writers
for decades had portrayed as almost standing still in time, therefore
became very appealing, especially when one could expect to find
the romantic scenery and hospitable welcome of literary legend.

Late nineteenth-century writers like Whitelaw Reid, Harriet
Beecher Stowe, Ledyard Bill, Sidney Lanier, George M. Barbour,
Charles Henry Webber, James W. Davidson, Henry M. Field, and
Bradford Torry, to mention only a few, had focused generations
of Americans' attention on Florida and fashioned an image of
paradise that still draws tourists every year.[2] Others, including Edward King in his well-received book entitled *The Great South* (1875),
published both in New York and London, focused on many places
throughout the entire South. King wrote euphemistically that nothing about Atlanta reminded him of the North. He mistakenly
described the Georgia capital as a place surrounded by "romantic,
moss-hung oaks . . . where the magnolias, the bay, and the palmetto vie with one another in the exquisite, inexplicable charm of
their voluptous beauty." Charleston was a town whose houses and
streets, "unlike [those] of any . . . new and smartly painted northern
town, . . . have an air of dignified repose and solidity." King reported that he wandered through Savannah "in a kind of dream,"
and while in Mobile, found a drive "along a quiet and secluded road
reminiscent of one rich bloom and the greenness of England." He
bragged that "in Florida the subtle moonlight, the perfect glory of
the dying sun, . . . the perfume faintly borne from the orange grove,
the murmurous music of waves along the inlets, and the mangrove
covered banks [of the St. Johns River] are beyond words." Finally,
King came to the untenable conclusion that the widely held belief
in Silver Springs as the Fountain of Youth appeared to be "firmly
founded" and that in the Everglades "some of the richest lands in
the world" lay idle and could be purchased for "a trifle."[3]

Almost forty years later, at the dawn of the automobile age, writers described the South in the same fascinating terms. To a gen-

eration of Americans seeking to reject the modern urban-industrial world by getting "back to nature" and seeking sanctuary in a rustic country haven, these romantic embellishments made the region appear much more exotic than backward. Witness how one writer in 1911 poetically described the South to readers of *Collier's Weekly*. "There are no nightingales in our South," he claimed, "but the mockingbirds sing in the March moonlight – moonlight as warm and tremulous with jasmine and with spring as any that Petrarch knew – and the thrush and redbird decorate the morning silences. In April the earth wakes in new green, in white dogwoods and gay azaleas as glorious as in any Italian wood, and with May the summer comes as sumptuously."[4]

This same uncritical romantic description of the South could be found in hundreds of articles written during the first two decades of the twentieth century for magazines like *Review of Reviews*, *American Mercury*, *Literary Digest*, *The Outlook*, *Survey*, *World's Work*, *Saturday Evening Post*, *Harper's Weekly*, and *Popular Mechanics*. In January 1912, for example, *Country Life in America* carried a story by Percy H. Whiting claiming that the South was not yet fully developed, was still "vast in extent, scattered in population, and only just beginning to recoup from the financial losses of war times and reconstruction." Nevertheless, he recommended motoring trips there without reservation and boasted that "despite all handicaps the people of the South have so improved their roads that they are perfectly 'possible' for touring purposes." Whiting made the solicitous point that, even if traveling conditions were less than desirable, those who loved nature and aspired to experience what life had to offer in a tropical wilderness should abandon their qualms and head south.[5]

A few years later, *Harper's* set another writer, Louise Closser Hale, accompanied by her husband and an illustrator, on a circuitous motor trip south from New York City through the state of Virginia. After her party passed a sign marking the Mason-Dixon line and the boundary between Pennsylvania and Maryland, her entire outlook on the trip changed. When Hale wrote that "the yellow paint and black lettering [of the road sign] stood for the warm things of life," the romantic interpretation given the South by writers for decades was showing its effect. "It [the sign] spoke of jasmine," she continued, "and mocking birds, turbaned slaves, old mahogany, low bows and ruffled shirt fronts."[6]

By 1925 this message was even being heard over the radio. George Elliott Cooley broadcast a weekly travelogue series entitled "Touring with a Packard Eight" from the New York City studios of WEAF. The way Cooley described the South gave his listeners the impression that, while the region may have once been impoverished and dilapidated, it was being rebuilt to retain its romance and rustic charm.[7] Obviously, when it came to the South, twentieth-century observers did not depart from the customary exaggerations. If anything, they offered readers and listeners an even more mythical version of the region to contemplate. The response, as we shall see, was overwhelming.

Contributing to the urge to drive into the South were improved and more easily obtainable route guides. The most widely used were those distributed by the AAA, which published its first in 1900. By 1910, when it put out its first official motoring guide to the South — the one Seymour Cunningham used — route guides remained somewhat of a novelty and definitely not something a motorist could rely upon for directions on a long, grueling trip. By today's standards these first road maps of the South were sketchy, essentially defining only the route that R. H. Johnston blazed in 1908 between Savannah and New York, and the one from Washington to Columbia, South Carolina, that Leonard Tufts called the Capital Highway.

The 1910 AAA guide that mapped the route from the Northeast into the Southeast detailed only a few of the towns that were situated within a few miles of the recommended highway.[8] In the years that followed, the AAA refined and updated its information and included roads in the various southern states that intersected the officially approved routes. Gradually, road maps of the South became better representations of the region rather than just a piece of paper with lines drawn between major population centers. This refinement gave travelers a better geographical understanding of the region and encouraged them to abandon – if only for a short time – the well-worn paths between cities and towns in the North and South. Before the end of World War I, private companies and other automobile clubs besides the AAA entered the touring guide publishing business. In 1918, for example, the Automobile Club of America (ACA) came out with its "Dixie Tour," which guided motorists from New York City over thirteen hundred miles through the South to Miami Beach. This impressive publication listed distances between towns and villages, recommended hotel accommodations in larger cities along the route, and made the important distinction between the roads that were more "improved" than others. That same year, the AAA's official motoring guide to the South, volume six of the *Automobile Blue Book*, contained directions for an unprecedented twenty-four thousand miles of roads through an unprecedented eight southern states.[9]

Complementing these detailed guides were articles about the South that the AAA and the ACA published in their widely read magazines, *American Motorist* and *Motor Travel*. These publications inevitably exhibited the same poular romantic imagery that had so characterized nineteenth-century books and articles about the South, as well as conscious appeals to motorists intrigued by nature. In 1920, one article about North Carolina in the *American Motorist*, for example, began by stating that "surely the soft lazy days of summer when Nature makes for man's enjoyment a wonderful garden of this region is the ideal time to visit. The pleasant valley of the St. Johns River, . . . the sylvan beauty of the deep hemlock coves and the gorgeous views of the towering peaks of the Blue Ridge in the fiery glory of a summer's sunset afford a pleasure unalloyed to the lover of the beautiful and the sublime in Nature."[10]

Another 1920 article, in *Motor Travel*, referred to the South as "The Land of Perpetual Sunshine," and another maintained that a popular route through Georgia passed "through charming practically unknown country where the sleepy donkey and the equally lazy negro eke out an existence as picturesque and as primitive as that bequeathed to them by the early Jesuits." In 1913 and 1918, Henry MacNair, one-time editor of the AAA's *Blue Book*, wrote articles for *Travel* in which he stated that it was a mistake to overlook the rest of the South when motoring to Florida. In addition to pointing out how charming and quaint the region was, he concluded that, where only a few years ago motorists had approached a trip into the southern United States with great trepidation, "a sortie through the southland [in 1918] was no longer considered a perilous adventure."[11]

In only a few short years, writers who had extolled the South's romanticism were telling Americans that southerners were making it easier for them to enjoy the delights of blissful landscapes and pastoral scenery firsthand. In 1912, in order for the automobilist to turn "his back on the pallid [winter] landscape of the north" and "seek the home of spring or summer in the lands that lie in the south," a writer for *Harper's Weekly* proclaimed, he had to put his motor vehicle aboard a train or steamer and ship it to Charleston, Savannah, or a port city on Florida's east coast. By 1920, the train, as one writer noted, was no longer necessary. Florida, he claimed, no longer lay "beyond arduous and impassable sands, behind impenetrable morasses of red gumbo and just around the corner from Stygian cypress swamps and other road unpleasantries."[12] Interstate highways had made paradise seem one hundred miles closer to the northern motorist.

With the South now reportedly more accessible, newspaper and magazine writers layered their descriptions of the South with the same thick, syrupy romanticism. The one writer who departed more than most from this long-established practice of image-making was Kenneth Lewis Roberts. Roberts gained recognition later as an historical novelist, but in the early 1920s he was credited with initiating what became popularly known as "the Florida boom." In 1921, Roberts was stationed in Washington as a congressional correspondent for the *Saturday Evening Post*, an assignment he regarded with little enthusiasm. Not one to hide his feelings, he made his dissatisfaction known to *Post* editor George Horace Lorimer, who granted him a reprieve and sent him on a month-long trip to Miami Beach to write a series of stories about the experiences of vacationers from the North. What Roberts found, as he later recalled in his autobiography, was few northern vacationers, "a desert waste beach of pumped-in sand, a checkerboard [town] of unpopulated avenues," and less than a half-dozen hotels catering to tourists.[13] He chose, however, not to reveal any of these facts but instead to portray Florida essentially the way its boosters wanted: as an emerging oasis, no longer enjoyed only by the privileged few but by middle- and working-class Americans.

In his three initial *Post* articles about Florida that appeared during the spring of 1922, Roberts made only casual reference to the state's mysticism but wrote convincingly about improved roads in the South and the fact that small, low-cost automobiles had made the Land of Sunshine accessible to almost everyone. His conclusion that Palm Beach was popular because of its democracy challenged the notion that south Florida was strictly a rich man's paradise. "A Philadelphia Biddle," he observed, "is just as apt as not to come along and accidentally rub damp sand on a South Bend Smith."

From Roberts's articles we get a glimpse of the kind of tourists who were attracted to making the long, grueling trip through the South by automobile to Florida, as well as an explanation of why they came. For example, Roberts wrote about a dairyman from Sandusky, Ohio, whom he met in south Florida. The man confided to Roberts that he "had grown tired of developing rheumatism, chilblains, and a grouch during the long winter months" and decided to come to Florida. Roberts also mentioned an Indiana farmer who had motored to Florida because "he preferred sitting around where it was comfortably warm to sitting around where it was uncomfortably cold." Roberts called these people "sun-hunters," men and women who did not want to wait for "April to come along and unstiffen [their] joints." They chose instead, he claimed, to spend the winter "amid the Spanish moss and palm trees, harkening dreamily to the cheerful twittering of dicky-birds and to the stirring thuds of coconuts, oranges, and grapefruits as they [fell] heavily to the ground."[14]

Roberts paid at least three other visits to Florida. And in addition to his eleven articles in the *Saturday Evening Post* between 1922 and 1926, he wrote three books about the state, *Sun Hunting* (1922), *Florida Loafing* (1925), and *Florida* (1926). None of his books became as popular as his *Post* articles, nor did they disseminate as well the message that Florida had finally become what writers had been describing for decades: an accessible paradise. But Roberts, better than any of his contemporaries, sold twentieth-century Americans on the belief that, no matter what their profession, assets, or status in life, Florida was for them. He argued with confidence that, in the previous forty years, few Americans had been able to travel, but in that short time, the affordable automobile had been produced, and southern roads had been improved enough to make a motoring excursion feasible.[15]

Roberts also wrote extensively and persuasively about another tangible Florida attraction: the chance to get rich quick in real estate. Between 1922 and 1925, newspapers and magazines across the country reported stories of men who made overnight fortunes buying and selling land in Florida. This provided an additional inducement to Americans contemplating a trip south, and to some this was an even better reason to come to Florida than merely to enjoy the climate. In 1923–24, when he made his second trip to Palm Beach, Roberts confirmed these boom stories and gave credibility to the widely held notion that little or no money was needed to speculate in Florida real estate. "Frequently true stories . . . have gone out from Florida for three years or more," he wrote in the spring of 1924

> to the effect that Mr. James P. Grimp bought a piece of Palm Beach land for $3.50 and sold it for $250,000; that Miss Effie Ribble bought five acres in St. Petersburg for $100 and disposed of them for $100,000; that business property in Miami, worth $1,286 some eight years ago, was now selling for $60,000 a front inch; that 911 persons had become millionaires out of Tampa real estate in the last seven days; that any piece of real estate bought anywhere in Florida increased 100 per cent in value every twenty-nine hours; and so on and so forth.[16]

Roberts later assumed the blame for starting and spreading these far-fetched rumors of average Americans becoming fabulously wealthy overnight, but the attention he gave to yet another Florida phenomenon proved ultimately to be as much of an enticement to prospective tourists as the tales he related about the unprecedented prospects of wealth. In his *Post* stories, Roberts introduced Americans to working people like themselves – dairymen, farmers, carpenters, tile setters, masons, bricklayers, druggists, and small shop owners – who had seemingly dropped everything at home and gone, by automobile, to Florida. Relying on amusing stories and satire more often than on the familiar romantic hyperbole, which remained popular with other journalists who covered the state, Roberts gave readers a seemingly more objective view of the Florida boom and a picture of the everyday people who participated in it. His descriptions of average men and women enjoying the winter months in Florida enabled readers to relate to what was happening there. Both Roberts and *Post* editor George Lorimer halfway assumed responsibility for the phenomenal overnight popularity of the state. The Florida craze of the 1920s, however, had roots that went back to Reconstruction, and Roberts's vital contribution was that he reported the Florida boom like no other journalist. If nothing else, he caused Americans to think seriously about driving their automobiles south.

These less-than-affluent but highly mobile Americans comprised a new fraternity of automobile tourists who traveled quite differently from earlier motorists like Seymour Cunningham and his family. Touring by motor vehicle offered these travelers a freedom from fixed itineraries, rigid schedules, and inflexible timetables. The low-cost automobile and improved tourist highways had made it possible for persons of modest means to go where they wanted, when they wanted, and at the pace they wanted. Cunningham's 1910 trip from Connecticut to South Carolina gave a hint of this, but it was not until after World War I that this style of travel became more popular in America. United by shared motoring experiences, the lure of life in the outdoors, and a sense of roadside democracy, the postwar vagabond auto tourists carried all of their necessities with them, strapped and wired to every conceivable surface of their mud-spattered, dusty vehicles.

A typical automobile might have a knock-down tent and suit-cases attached to one running board, and collapsible beds, accor-dion mattresses, a come-apart stove, and a telescopic dishwasher tied to the other. Beneath a false floor in the tonneau were kitchen utensils, tables, folding chairs, water buckets, and all the culinary necessities that might somehow be needed. Canned goods were placed under the seat, slung against the top, packed along the sides, tucked beneath the cushions, and stacked along the floor in such number that, in many cases, they so increased the weight of the car that driving over unimproved muddy or sandy roads was much more difficult. After a hard day on the road, the autocamper ex-tended the tent at a right angle from the side door of the vehicle, heated a can of beans on the car radiator, and made use of the automobile as a combination lavatory, sitting room, chiffonier, clothes closet, pantry, and safe-deposit vault. But while careful plan-ning and all the right camping equipment for rough-and-tumble excursions were the concerns of some motorists, to many unable to afford these on-the-road luxuries, a few pots and pans and a cou-ple of blankets tossed in the back seat, along with a strip of canvas to stretch between the car and two stakes at night for shelter, were all that was needed. Roberts reported that some cars were laden with so much gear and equipment that they looked swollen out of recognition and could have as easily made a "dash for the Pole" as the trek to not-so-distant Miami Beach.

With no public camping facilities available at first, a place to stop for the night was an everyday problem while on the road. Some weary motorists set up camp on private property, with or without owners' permission; others found a church or school yard, or per-haps even a cemetery in which to spend the night. Not all motorists, however, were as tidy as many rural southerners wanted them to be. Autocampers often littered the roadside with their garbage, left their campsites in worse condition than they found them, tore down farmers' fences for firewood, and sometimes even carelessly started destructive fires. Before long, the out-of-state motorist gained the unsavory reputation of an automobile hobo and began to experience even more difficulty finding a place to stop overnight.[17]

Glad to have escaped the harsh northern winter, tin-can tourists from Ohio enjoy the mild climate in Tampa at Florida's first municipal autocamp, ca. 1921. The camp opened in December 1919 on the banks of the Hillsborough River in DeSoto Park. Courtesy of the Hillsborough County, Florida, Public Library.

This led to the beginning of two institutions in the South: the first motorized campers' club organized in the United States and the opening of the first automobile tourist camps, forerunners to the motel. In December 1919, twenty-one autocampers, led by James M. Morrison of Chicago, convened on the banks of the Hillsborough River in Tampa's DeSoto Park. They had been attracted there when Tampa business leaders, in hopes of augmenting tourism, convinced municipal officials to open the park for free to all out-of-state motor tourists. Morrison and his friends wanted to give the growing contingent of autocampers a better reputation and came to the conclusion that an association to represent their interests and to present them to the public in a better light was necessary. The result was the organization of the Tin Can Tourists of the World (TCT), which took its name from the tin-can items these campers carried with them during the winter months when they were unable to purchase fresh vegetables and other necessary supplies from roadside vendors. In April of 1922, the TCT claimed to have attracted thirty thousand members, who identified one another by an empty tin can turned upside down atop the car radiator. Incorporated within the TCT's constitution, adopted in January 1920, was an agreement sworn to by members "to leave all camp grounds clear, leave no fires, destroy no property, . . . purloin nothing and [to] conduct [themselves] in a manner creditable to the T.C.T."

The winter of 1919–20 saw only a few autocampers in Florida, but during the following few years, their number was counted in the thousands. Two years later, during the winter of 1921–22, an unprecedented 4,329 out-of-state tourists and their 1,571 motor vehicles packed DeSoto Park in Tampa to its very limits, and George W. Simmons, Jr., Florida's chief sanitary engineer, estimated that approximately 10,000 auto tourists spent a portion if not the entire winter in the state. Although roadside camps sprang up more slowly along the well-traveled highways leading through southern states than in Michigan, Wisconsin, or even Colorado, before long, hundreds of autocamps were in operation throughout the South. At the end of 1921 there were thirty-eight established autocamps in Florida, thirty of which were maintained by municipalities and the remainder by private individuals. All of these were located on the well-traveled interstate highways leading into the state: from Jacksonville to Miami on the east coast, from New Port Richey to Sarasota on the Gulf coast, and from Lake City to Dade City in the interior. Three years later the number of autocamps in Florida grew to 95, and by the spring of 1926, 210 were in operation and served an estimated 125,000 motorized tourists annually.[18]

Occasionally, these camping communities, like DeSoto Park in Tampa, Lemon City on the outskirts of Miami, and another facility opened in 1921 by the city of West Palm Beach in an area originally designated as a city park, operated either without charging its patrons or by charging them nominally. The idea was to attract tourists, and communities went to great lengths to do just that. Well-organized citizens' committees routinely greeted out-of-state motorists as they rolled into town, and at first some of the larger Florida camps provided guests with police protection, nightly entertainment, electric lights, oyster roasts, hot running water, showers, city sewage, and streetcar service to town—all free of charge.[19]

In the case of West Palm Beach, a wayward autocamper even had access to a building on the grounds of the camp which contained a modern Piggly Wiggly–style grocery store; a meat market; a dry goods counter; a drug counter; a four-table poolroom; a restaurant; a post office; a newsstand; and a gasoline, tire, and oil accessory store. West Palm Beach built this camp during 1924 when the city park, the site of its original facility, became overcrowded. The city constructed this second camp, known as Bacon Park, southwest of town on an old lake bottom that had been drained when one of Lake Okeechobee's canals was completed. Operation of the camp was governed by city ordinance, and during 1926, Bacon Park served approximately four thousand people who generated more than fifteen thousand dollars every month in revenue for the city.

Depending on their taste and budget, out-of-state motorists who enjoyed the accommodations at Bacon Park had a choice of three types of facilities: a bungalow, a tent house, or a wooden-floor tent. The most expensive of these, a comfortable fourteen-by-twenty-eight-foot bungalow, rented for a reasonable sixty-five dollars a month. In all there were eighty-four of these bungalows available for rent, each with a living room, a bedroom, a bathroom, and a kitchen. All windows were screened, and the bathroom furnishings consisted of a standard low tank-top porcelain toilet, a lavatory, and a shower stall with a concrete floor. In the living room were a large wicker table, two cane rocking chairs, and a day couch bed. The bedroom was furnished with a double-steel bed complete with two pillows and a mattress, a dresser, and six unpainted chairs. The kitchen featured a three-burner oil stove, a twenty-five-pound-capacity refrigerator, and a drop-leaf table. Each bungalow was also equipped with pans, kettles, cups, saucers, plates, knives, forks, spoons, galvanized washtub, brass washboard, sheets, towels, blankets, pillowcases, ironing board, and kerosene lamps.

In addition to these bungalows were sixty-eight "close to nature" tent houses. These were smaller and designed to suit motorists on tighter budgets as well as those who wanted more direct contact with the outdoors. Each of these frame units, which rented for between thirty and thirty-five dollars a month, sat on a wooden floor and was covered by a canvas screen. In case of inclement weather, this screen could be drawn from the inside. Each tent house was furnished with a double bed and mattress, four chairs, one table, a three-burner oil stove, a refrigerator, and a kerosene lantern. Although there was no running water in any of these houses, at the rear of each unit tourists had access to a water main and a catch basin connected to the sewer. For even less money—five dollars a week—visitors to Bacon Park could rent one of a hundred tents which also sat on wooden floors. These facilities were equipped similarly to the tent houses, but unlike the bungalows, had no private baths. Thus, for a very nominal amount of money, an entire family could come to Florida for the winter and camp out under swaying palms and romantic moonlight. They could, in other words, become part of the romantic country life myth and not just armchair dreamers who had made "literary commuting" so popular in America.[20]

America's involvement in World War I temporarily slowed the flow of motor tourists to the South. During the war years of 1917 to 1919, some Americans braved the risks of poor roads to visit friends and relatives stationed at Army camps scattered across the region, but the allocation of steel, iron, and rubber to wartime needs by the War Industries Board halted the manufacture of touring cars and, for a time, curtailed tourism. At the end of 1919, passenger car production returned to normal, and Americans purchased automobiles like never before.[21] Although no official statistics exist that reveal the exact number of motorists, some from as far away as Canada, who came into the South during the heyday of this early twentieth-century motorized migration, several sources document the phenomenon unofficially. In December 1922, the *Literary Digest* quoted the secretary of the Jacksonville (Florida) Motor Club, who claimed to have kept monthly records of the out-of-the-state automobiles that entered Florida through Jacksonville. His figures indicated that in 1922, 80,640 motor vehicles came down the Dixie Highway and crossed the St. Johns River Bridge in downtown Jacksonville on their way south to St. Augustine, Ormond Beach, and points south. The popular weekly magazine stated that an additional 20,160 cars entered the state via other cities, making an estimated total of 100,800 out-of-state vehicles that came to Florida in 1922. The following year, Floridians estimated that the throng of out-of-state motorists who spent the winter months in their state spent an estimated $300,000,000.[22]

A year later, during the months of November and December 1924 and January 1925, 33,611 cars, from every state in the Union, were counted as they passed through downtown Jacksonville. Another 8,402 arrived on routes that led into the state through cities like Pensacola and Lake City, which brought the total number of motorists who came to Florida in just ninety days to over forty-two thousand. Considering those who came in 1924 by rail and boat, this put the annual number of visitors at well over one million. The following year, 1925, the motorized assault on paradise mushroomed even more. One writer who visited a tourist camp on one of the main highways leading to Florida estimated that during the winter and spring months of 1925 one hundred cars passed by each day. As the weather improved and as the roads became less treacherous, he said, this number increased to over two hundred a day, which was the case well into October, when rain and colder temperatures made traveling by automobile more uncomfortable than it already was.[23]

In 1925, approximately 500,000 motor vehicles rumbled into
the South from the other parts of the country over routes promoted
by highway progressives like J. Asa Rountree, Carl Fisher, and
Leonard Tufts. Many of these first-time visitors to the South were
on their way to Florida; and considering that each one of the cars
they drove carried an average of 3.6 persons, this made the number
of non-southerners who traveled by automobile through the southern
United States in 1925 alone easily exceed 1.9 million.[24] From
1920, when public auto tourist camps began opening in Florida
and along the major routes leading there, until 1926, when a
powerful hurricane put an end to the boom, an estimated four to
five million automobile tourists traveled through the South. This
annual transmigration of Americans from North to South and back
again by automobile, as we have seen, captured national attention
and even inspired one astute observer to respond poetically:

> It squeaked and groaned; 'twas rusty worn;
> Its fenders bent, its curtains torn,
> Its windshield cracked, its wheels not mates,
> Caked with mud of seven states,
> Headed South.[25]

Liberated by their automobiles and motivated by their steadfast
adherence to the doctrines of country life and back-to-nature movements, hundreds of thousands of Americans during the early 1920s
responded to the romantic claims they had heard about Florida
by heading south. The result was what one observer called a "pneumatic hegira" whose effects he compared to the descent of the Goths
on Rome, the Mongols on China, the Dutch on South Africa, and
the Mormon trek from Illinois to Utah.[26] "Cars poured out of side
streets and back roads onto the state roads in every part of the country," recalled another reporter,

> and roared along the state roads to the main travelled highways that led to
> the southeastern corner of the United States. Hour after hour, day after day,
> week after week, month after month, the roads between southern Florida and
> Washington, where the many highways of the northern most states converge
> into the Florida road, [appeared to be] an artificial serpent 1500 miles in length;

an endless serpent whose joints, composed entirely of automobiles, slipped easily over the ground in some spots and labored more violently in others, but on the whole managed to wiggle forward for a rate of thirty miles an hour.[27]

In the five decades between the end of the Civil War and the beginning of World War I, the numerous writers, artists, and illustrators who depicted Florida as a recreational haven did not directly change it or the South. What did bring about change was the actual throng of automobile tourists attracted by the region's greater accessibility, which highway progressivism had made possible. As motorists drove through the South on their way to Florida, their annual assault on paradise also had a lasting and revolutionary cultural impact on the region and its people. Once southerners found automobile tourism to be of great economic importance, the South lost some of its regional distinctiveness and, as we shall see, began to conform to more national cultural standards.

Farmscape into Roadscape

During the 1920s, Americans, in mud-spattered motor vehicles whose windshields were often cracked from the torturous conditions of southern roads and whose fenders were rarely free of dents, could be found on at least a dozen interstate highways that connected the South with other parts of the country. As these early motorists stopped along the highway to refuel, ask directions, visit a site of historical significance, resupply depleted provisions, stay the night in an autocamp or tourist home, or simply chat with local residents about the weather and road conditions, long-established daily routines were interrupted and cultural changes resulted. These changes made the region less provincial and more like the rest of the nation. The natural environment became so intertwined with the material culture of automobility that an entirely new cultural landscape emerged to serve the needs of people who were between one place and another. During the 1920s and 1930s, the most visible and tangible signs of change in the rural South were along the highways where the burgeoning new automobile tourist economy first developed.

This new roadscape was distinctively and unmistakably American and proved to be the most visible evidence of the revolutionary change that the combination of highway progressivism and automobility brought to the South. The highways that stretched from Dixie into other parts of the country, therefore, were not only a means by which tourists came into the South but avenues for cultural

change. Perhaps President Woodrow Wilson, a transplanted
southerner himself, best understood what was about to happen.
On the eve of the massive automobile tourism that the South experienced during the early 1920s, Wilson responded to a letter he
had received from Dr. Samuel M. Johnson, director of the Robert
E. Lee Highway Association. "It is a happy old saying," the president wrote in January 1921, "that sectional lines are obliterated only
by the feet who cross them, and [the Lee Highway] should con-
tribute to that much-to-be-desired result."[1]

Where motorists who planned trips into the Southland resided—
whether in New England, the Middle Atlantic states, the West,
the Midwest, or even Canada—determined which route they would
take. By the mid-1920s, there were twelve widely known interstate
highways into the South. From the District of Columbia to Atlanta,
one of the most popular and well-traveled roads, the Bankhead National Highway, remained essentially the same route that R. H.
"Pathfinder" Johnston blazed in the fall of 1908. West of Atlanta,
it wound through the Deep South states of Alabama, Mississippi,
and Louisiana until it stretched all the way to San Diego, California. The other most traveled route was the well-publicized Dixie
Highway. It led motor tourists out of Detroit, Chicago, and other
midwestern cities and towns to Carl Fisher's renowned "paradise"
at Miami Beach. The Atlantic Coastal Highway, or Ocean Highway
as it was later called, also terminated at Miami, but it began in
Quebec City, Canada, and ran along the eastern seaboard through
New England to New York City and Philadelphia. Once it crossed
the Mason-Dixon line, it veered to the east and then turned south
down the Atlantic coast to Florida. Not far west of the Atlantic
Coastal Highway was Leonard Tufts's inspiration, the Capital
Highway. It connected the District of Columbia with the state
capitals of Virginia, North Carolina, and South Carolina; and of
course, it passed within close proximity to Tufts's growing resort
at Pinehurst. Another popular route, the Lee Highway, began in
New York City, passed through the District of Columbia, western
Virginia, eastern Tennessee, and Birmingham, Alabama, before it

reached New Orleans, its southernmost point. In the Crescent City, it became the Robert E. Lee Transcontinental Highway and connected the West Coast cities of San Francisco, Los Angeles, and San Diego with the southern United States. Other routes familiar to motorists were the Jefferson Davis Highway, which linked the distant cities of Winnipeg and Manitoba with New Orleans; the Jackson Highway, which started in Cincinnati and also ended in New Orleans; the Mississippi River Scenic Highway from Winnepeg to Ft. Myers, Florida; and the Old Spanish Trail, which traversed the continent from St. Augustine, Florida, to San Diego.[2]

By 1924 this network of privately inspired interstate highways that crisscrossed the South, as well as others throughout the nation, had become so complex that the American Association of State Highway Officials petitioned the United States Department of Agriculture to alleviate the situation by instituting some kind of numbering system. The following year, the Joint Board of State and Federal Highway Officials was created and, within eighteen months, came up with a solution. In November 1926, the joint board held a meeting at Leonard Tufts's resort at Pinehurst, North Carolina. In attendance were many prominent public officials representing all governmental levels, including Secretary of Agriculture William M. Jardine, North Carolina Governor Angus W. McLean, and North Carolina Highway Commissioner Frank Page.

As president of the American Association of State Highway Officials, Page made the organization's new plan public. It called for the designation of all east-west interstate highways with even numbers and all north-south routes with odd numbers. U.S. highways 10, 20, 30, and 40 stretched westward across the northern half of the nation, and highways 50, 60, 70, 72, 74, 78, 80, and 90 ran east-west through the southern states. Generally the numbers given to north-south highways were lower than fifty, but because many of these highways intersected and sometimes merged with one another, it was impossible for the board to give a particular highway any certain number. Much but not all of the Capital Highway, for example, became U.S. 1; U.S. 17, for the most part, was the Atlantic Coastal Highway; the Dixie Highway, with its

The American Tourist Camp, located on U.S. 1 near Henderson, North Carolina, offered weary motorists a variety of roadside conveniences, including a tea room and overnight accommodations with private baths, ca. 1935. U.S. 1 was the same route Leonard Tufts had earlier promoted as the Capital Highway. Courtesy of the Library of Congress.

dual routes through the South, became U.S. 41, U.S. 27, U.S. 25, and U.S. 441; through Mississippi, Alabama, and Georgia, the Dixie Overland Highway was assigned the number U.S. 80; and farther south the Old Spanish Trail, which originally terminated in St. Augustine and now ended in Jacksonville, was given the number U.S. 90 as its official designation.[3] (See map 6.)

Therefore, by 1927, a new classification for the nation's highways was in place, and the many routes that ran throughout the South became absorbed into the new national interstate network. National standardized black-and-white signs in the form of a shield emblazoned with the route number in the center replaced the colorful and regionally identifiable route markers that had at first marked the course of the many highways leading through the South. Stretches of roads and streets leading in and out of some cities and towns in the South still bear the names "Dixie Highway," "Bankhead Highway," or "Lee Highway," but for the most part, these routes have lost their once regionally distinctive designations, and their importance to the development of the twentieth-century South has been forgotten.

Important as they were to opening the South to the outside world, the interstate highways that crisscrossed the southern United States and served as conduits for countless pleasure-seekers were more than just a means of access. The new highway culture that emerged to serve the new tourist economy had a tremendous effect on numerous small southern towns through which these routes passed. As a general rule, small towns in the South that were not served by an interstate highway faced uncertain futures. Unlike towns born during the nineteenth century as a direct result of railroad construction, very few towns or villages in the South came about because of a highway. Overgrown tourist camps—like the unincorporated village of Lakeview, North Carolina, located on U.S. 1 between Sanford and Southern Pines, which came into being to serve motor tourists—were the unquestioned inventions of the road. With its assortment of filling stations, tourist cabins, as well as picnic grounds, Lakeview took both its identity and its economic existence from

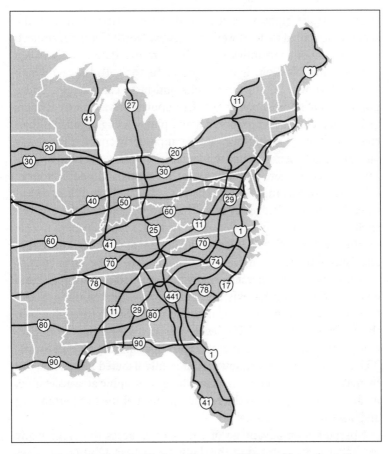

Map 6. Eastern half of the National Interstate Highway Network, 1926.

the highway. Some established towns, like Swainsboro, Georgia, located at the intersection of U.S. 1 and U.S. 80, grew from sleepy nineteenth-century villages and thrived on the economic stimulus these interstate routes provided. And still other communities, like Cocoa, Florida, also located on U.S. 1, just south of Titusville, could credit their twentieth-century survival to the boon of automobile tourism.

But at the same time that these communities with direct access to an interstate highway seemed to flourish, others located on the same routes failed to do as well. Ridgeway, North Carolina, situated on U.S. 1 about ten miles from the Virginia state line, between Manson and Norlina, is an example. In 1938, Ridgeway, which was well known for its sumptuous and tasty cantaloupes, had a population of approximately 250. Its population was mostly farmers of German descent who worked small plots raising vegetables, berries, and fruits. The highway at first apparently enabled Ridgeway farmers to get their produce to market in Virginia and North Carolina, but when there was a bad year for crops and people sought other ways of earning a living, the road also facilitated their departure, thus erasing Ridgeway from the map.[4] Therefore, the progressive argument that improved roads would enable farmers to stay on the farm while they enjoyed the ability to escape its drudgery and isolation proved at least in this instance to be erroneous.

The presence of interstate highways also caused lasting cultural changes in the South's existing small towns. Spartanburg, South Carolina, was one of many small towns in the South through which the Bankhead National Highway passed. In fact, once the route entered the city limits, it merged with Spartanburg's Main Street. The highway's presence, however, not only ushered in tourists, but by making a wider and more immediate geographic area accessible, it caused a disruption to the routine pattern of life in Spartanburg and its surrounding area.

Spartans took advantage of this greater accessibility in many ways that were reflected in the daily newspaper. Obituary notices listed deaths in communities as far away as thirty miles; Spartanburg civic organizations and women's clubs included members from outlying towns and villages; churches in surrounding towns advertised their Sunday services as if they were as centrally located as the First Baptist Church on Main Street; and nearby communities held sporting events that brought together residents from the entire county and beyond. In the spring of 1928, for example, the Central Textile Baseball League was organized in Spartanburg County. The league at first included four clubs representing the small communities of Drayton, Cowpens, Fingerville, and Glendale. Within five years, sixteen additional teams had joined the county league. Teams traveled from community to community within the county, playing a rigorous schedule that began in April and concluded in August.[5] Without the mobility that road improvements provided, none of this would have been possible.

Although it would be decades before the viability of the traditional cores of many small southern towns like Spartanburg would

When Farm Security Administration photographer Walker Evans made this picture of Main Street in downtown Macon, Georgia, in March 1936, the main focus of economic activity had not yet been shifted away by the incoming Dixie Highway to the outskirts of town. Courtesy of the Library of Congress.

lose their commercial appeal entirely, the process of decline began during the 1920s, when residents became more mobile and automobile tourism increased. By 1935, town squares like Spartanburg's historic Morgan Square, named after American Revolutionary War hero General Daniel Morgan, were forced to share the spotlight of economic activity with interstate highways that stretched in from the adjacent countryside. The incoming highway, with its ever-present conglomeration of billboards, service stations, and tourist facilities, gradually drained away small towns' economic vitality and slowly redirected the community's civic focus. Where the nineteenth-century railroad station once served as a means of entrance to town, during the twentieth century the modern highway assumed a similar function. And, as geographer John A. Jakle has observed, "the highway turned the old order around."[6]

Where the town square had once welcomed outsiders stepping off the train, visitors who came by automobile first encountered a town's outskirts. Within a few years, as traffic became congested on main streets, merchants began to lose more money than the increased accessibility generated. To alleviate this problem, local governments constructed routes that circumvented towns. This temporarily solved the traffic problem, but at the same time, it began to shift the focus of commerce away from the traditional hub of activity on main street to the outskirts of town. Eventually, these communities assumed the familiar identity of every other American small town along the monotonous interstate highway: a place synonymous with overnight tourist accommodations, hot meals, and a quick fill-up.

As small towns in the South began to stretch out along interstate highways to greet incoming tourists, southerners began to realize new commerical opportunities that the emerging national automobile culture dictated. Motor vehicles needed fuel, oil, spare parts, garage accommodations and, when trouble occurred, qualified mechanics. At first, motorists generally aided one another when mechanical failures happened, but breakdowns and mishaps were so common that "gipsy repairmen" began to appear along the most frequently traveled routes leading south.[7] These mobile repairmen, however, were few and often unable to handle the crippling mechanical troubles that many automobile tourists of that era experienced. Stranded by broken axles, shattered suspension systems, cracked steering assemblies, smashed drive trains, punctured radiators, stripped gears, overheated engines, and a host of other serious difficulties common to automobiles of that vintage, desperate motorists created a demand for the sale of standardized automobile parts and for garages with qualified mechanics.

Whether it was a repair part or a mechanic that they desperately needed, tourists expected to find the same consumer goods and services they enjoyed at home. This demand greatly influenced national companies that supplied accessories and repair parts to begin for the first time to sell their merchandise below the Mason-Dixon line. National manufacturers, including the Goodyear Tire and Rubber Company and the Prest-O-Lite Battery Company, opened dealerships in Atlanta and distributed their merchandise to owners of general stores and other retailers who operated businesses in small towns and communities throughout the South. And if a merchant did not have a particular part in stock, it could be ordered from a catalog.

The two things motorists could not buy out of a catalog, however, were gasoline and motor oil. As a rule, traditional general stores and livery stables in the South were the first to sell these necessities to the public. General-store owners installed curbside gasoline pumps at which passing motorists could stop and fill their tanks. Motor oil was dispensed in five-gallon cans from large storage barrels outside these same stores.[8] As tourism increased and more and more local citizens purchased motor vehicles, safety and convenience dictated the means of supplying consumer demand. Some general-store operators installed underground storage tanks and moved gasoline pumps away from buildings. Others opened independent filling stations and added adjacent autocamps to attract customers. One such facility, located just east of Williamsburg, Virginia, was operated by W. E. Topping, president of the locally owned Topping Oil Company. The combination service station and autocamp stood on the ground formerly occupied by Fort Magruder and was in itself a citadel of roadside modernization. The camp contained twenty-six separate cabins, each equipped with hot and cold running water, a playground for children, public restrooms with showers, a dining room, and a connecting reception room where tourists congregated. Adjacent to the camp was a gasoline service station, one of thirty Topping owned in the area, all of which were supplied by Shell Eastern Petroleum Products.[9]

It was not long before national oil companies began selling their products directly to the motoring public in the South rather than through independent operators like Topping. As demand increased, especially on the interstate highways between the North and South, these national corporations erected filling stations along highways on the outskirts of communities. Their stations, often the most prominent physical landmarks along the highway leading into town, were standard in appearance and displayed logos recognized from coast to coast. Among the first national oil companies to begin retail sales in the South was the Gulf Refining Company of Pittsburgh, Pennsylvania. Gulf did business in the South through its headquarters in Atlanta, which opened in 1907. Kerosene, or "Lusterlite" as it was known in Florida, was Gulf's principal product. It was shipped from the refinery to terminals in Tampa and Jacksonville, Florida. From there it went out by railroad tank car to company distributors or independent jobbers throughout the Southeast. The distributor stored the kerosene in a holding tank from which he sold it wholesale to retail establishments in towns and communities within about a twenty-mile radius. These included private garages, corner grocery and feed stores, hardware and paint dealers, blacksmith shops, livery stables, bicycle dealers, general stores, and other retailers that sold petroleum products. Deliveries were made by mule- or horse-drawn tank wagon, and until 1941, when the Southeastern Pipeline was completed, Gulf distributed its gasoline and other associated oil products this same way, except that tank trucks instead of mule-powered wagons were used. From a bulk storage tank, store owners then dispensed the petroleum in five-gallon cans or tins, which, as a rule, filled most early gasoline-powered motor vehicles' tanks to capacity.[10]

Although companies like Standard Oil of California sold gasoline directly to motorists as early as 1905, Gulf did not enter what was to become the very lucrative retail market until 1913. That year Gulf constructed its first experimental drive-in service station in Pittsburgh, Pennsylvania, and began what became a long-lasting practice of giving road maps of the United States to its customers, free of charge. Eight years later, about the same time automobile tourism was on the rise, the company began opening service stations in the South and, by 1926, operated 125 facilities in the states of Georgia, Florida, North and South Carolina. It was common practice, when a customer pulled into a station to purchase gasoline, for the station attendant to check under the hood of the car. Because Gulf found that in the South many customers objected to having the hoods of their cars raised without permission, Gulf instructed its employees to perform this service only upon request. Another accommodation to the South that Gulf made was in the design of a number of its stations. For stations that catered to more commerical than pleasure vehicles, the rule of thumb was to build the shed above the gasoline pumps high enough to allow a truck loaded to capacity with cotton bales to pass under unobstructed.[11]

Station design was also important because motorists intially recognized different oil companies as much by a familiar logo as by the way the station looked. In 1914, Standard Oil of California built its first thirty-four gasoline stations. They were small in size and uniform in appearance. It was not until 1922 that Gulf began to identify itself publicly by putting blue block-letters on an orange disc over its stations. In the South, in addition to this logo, the company adopted a standard white-brick-and-stucco architectural style that was prefabricated, relatively cheap to construct, and easily modified to incorporate a double or single driveway. The design also included a decorative running-water fountain in the front of each station, which management believed gave the building a civic respectability and a more aesthetic appearance. Executives hoped that this feature would make the small stations more eye-appealing and negate some of the criticism heard from southerners living in nearby residential areas who complained about gasoline stations' ugly appearance. Gulf erected this type of station in the southern states wherever business justified but generally in towns no smaller than Macon or Rome, Georgia.

One of Gulf's major competitors in the South, the Texas Company, was also aware of product recognition via service-station design and entered into similar territorial marketing strategies. In 1922, the Texas Company embarked on a program intended to establish a pattern of similarity among the stations it operated in each of its three retail terriories: northern, western, and southern. The style selected for the South was termed "Type W." Prefabricated white stucco walls, simulated columns supporting each corner of the station as well as the service canopy, Romanesque urns at the capital of each column, and a slanted tile cornice connecting the columns at the roofline conveyed the idea of permanence and identified the Texas Company to motorists as they traveled across the South.[12]

Between 1920 and 1930 gasoline service stations, the first commercial structures in America built in response to private automobile ownership, sprang up not only in the South but nationwide to support the growing demands of motor vehicle owners. By the end of 1929, there were approximately 120,000 gasoline stations in the United States, over 30,000 of which the Census Bureau classified as belonging to a chain. In the southern states there were 3,210 chain stations, but by far, most of the gasoline service stations in the region were independently operated by owners who purchased their gasoline and automotive products from national oil companies like Gulf, Standard, Shell, or Texas.[13] Therefore, whether out-of-state motorists or local farmers bought their motor oil and gasoline from a corner grocery store, at a locally owned station, or at one Gulf owned and operated, there was some degree of product recognition on the part of the customer.

In addition to gasoline, motor oil, repair parts, and qualified service in the inevitable event of mechanical breakdown, motorists traveling in the South needed food and shelter. Given the poor

The Texas Company's first standard-design "filling station" was constructed on Washington Avenue in Houston, Texas, in 1916. This station was the forerunner of the popular "Southern" type of stations built throughout Texas and other southern states between 1916 and 1930. Characteristic was the self-contained canopy under which cars were serviced. Courtesy of Texaco, Inc.

condition of the roads, about two hundred miles was about as far as motorists could travel in a day. And how much money they budgeted for accommodations along the highway, and how close they wanted to get to "nature," determined the way they spent their off-road hours. The more rugged—like one traveler during the winter of 1919–20 who motored from Ormond Beach, Florida, north on the Atlantic Coastal Highway to Cape Cod and along the way bathed in creeks and streams—camped in tents wherever they could.[14] Some

Curbside gasoline pumps were common in cities throughout the South between 1910 and 1920. The storefront station, which preceded the popular
drive-through station, replaced livery stables, garages, and general stores
where gasoline was first sold retail. This particular station was in New
Orleans, ca. 1915. Courtesy of Texaco, Inc.

roughed it in rustic autocamps while others relaxed in more comfortable accommodations. As time passed, and especially during
rainy seasons, more and more tourists found camping out under
the stars less inviting than having a roof over their heads and came
to prefer a bed to an uncomfortable cot or stuffy sleeping bag. Beginning about 1925, besides roadside autocamps or expensive, formal
hotels, motorists traveling in the southern states could choose between two other types of lodgings: either a small cabin erected by
a tourist camp owner or a private home opened to travelers.

Because of the region's warmer climate and the tendency of

motorists who came to Florida during the winter to stay for several months at a time, the cottage-camp idea had its beginnings in the South. The popularity of national parks in the western United States, however, quickly gave rise to tourist camping facilities there, and these first permanent roadside motels generally outdistanced campgrounds and tourist courts in the South in their modern, more comfortable accommodations. The construction of modern, furnished tourist cottages, cabins, bungalettes, apartments, or "floored tents," as they were sometimes called, was slow to come to the South, and as late as 1933, University of Washington sociologist Jesse F. Steiner reported that "privately operated camps are seen at their best in the western states." Nevertheless, up and down the highways that connected the South with the rest of the nation, tourist camps, like one that welcomed motorists to Florida just across the state line at Crystal Springs, could be found. In some cases, the tourist bonanza gave rise to entire villages.[15]

Still, finding a suitable inexpensive place to stay for a few days was not as easy as it might seem. In 1925 when Gilbert S. Chandler, a tin-can tourist, rolled into Tallahassee, Florida, he found neither an autocamp nor a tourist court to accommodate him or any other wayward motorist in need of a place to spend the night. Realizing that he was staring opportunity in the face, Chandler decided to go in business for himself. He made a deal with the city of Tallahassee that, for one dollar a year, allowed him to lease seven acres of city-owned real estate within a few blocks of the capitol. In return, he agreed to purchase several old dilapidated buildings on the property. Chandler first converted the site into an autocamp, remodeling one of the buildings into a store, another into a laundry, another into a community house, and a fourth into a bathhouse. But instead of demolishing three other smaller buildings and an old cattle-barn, Chandler revamped them into tourist cabins. He wired each for electricity, and, reasoning that most tourists carried both beds and stoves with them, furnished each cabin with nothing more than a homemade table and bench. "Our place," he recalled in an article published in *Tourist Court Journal*, "was considered a very modern tourist camp in those boom days of Florida."

During the autumn and winter of 1925, Chandler did a brisk business, but by the following spring and summer when the boom went bust, his cabins were vacant more often than rented. When the advent of colder weather again brought tourists to Florida, business had picked up so much that, during the winter of 1926–27, Chandler decided to construct several more cabins. These new additions were nine by twelve feet in size, had a small window at each end for ventilation, and were furnished with more of the same homemade furniture, this time including a bed frame made out of one-by-six-inch boards and, as Chandler described it, "a cheap second hand coil spring and straw mattress." "This," he said, "was an unusual departure for a tourist camp and we were able to charge $1.00 per week for the cottages so luxuriously appointed." That winter Chandler kept his cabins rented continuously and did well enough to purchase a Model T Runabout.

During 1927 many road improvements were being made in Florida under Governor John Martin. One of these was the paving of a highway – probably U.S. 90 – that led into Tallahassee from the west. This made Chandler a little uneasy, because, as he wrote, "some live-wire [might] build cabins better than ours on this new highway." To prevent this, Chandler himself purchased real estate adjacent to the incoming highway. After he convinced the city to grant him a license to construct a new tourist camp there, he erected six new Spanish-type cottages and moved ten cabins from his first camp to the new location.

The newly paved highway brought in a host of new motorists, many of whom had traveled in the West. They told Chandler about the better tourist accommodations found there and that what the South had to offer paled by comparison. At about that same time, *Harper's Monthly Magazine* carried a story stating that "no one who lives and motors east of the Mississippi has seen [tourist cottages] at their best." One facility in El Paso, Texas, known as Camp Grande, for example, offered vacationing motorists the kind of furnishings and service more closely associated with a hotel. For five dollars a day, Camp Grande provided its guests with silverware, rugs, bed linens, running water, gas heat, and even maid and telephone service. Camp Grande also offered its guests the convenience of a large kitchen where meals could be prepared, a playground for children, and a community dance hall for entertainment. In an effort to keep pace, Chandler spent an additional four thousand dollars to construct ten new cabins, all with private baths. "Still," he wrote, "we hated to see cars drive up with California license plates. They would inevitably say, 'In the West, they have such beautiful tourist courts, tile baths, inner-spring mattresses, garages and everything and *all* for a dollar.'"

These "modern" tourist cabins, found on U.S. 1 near Laurel, Maryland, and others like them, were the forerunners of the popular motel of today. Jack Delano made this photograph for the Farm Security Administration in June 1940. Courtesy of the Library of Congress.

After years of listening to his guests laud the tourist accommodations in the western states, Chandler made a motor excursion in
1936 through Texas, New Mexico, Arizona, and California to gain
first-hand knowledge of the tourist trade there. One of his first stops
was in Dallas at a $300,000 tourist court called the Grande Tourist
Lodges. Each night there cost him an unheard-of $7, but Chandler
deemed the expense well worth it. His western trip was an eye-
opening experience, and when he returned to Tallahassee, he entered
another phase in the development of his own facility. This time
Chandler constructed twenty sturdy cabins, all with fireproof as-
bestos or tile roofs, private tile baths with built-in tubs and showers,
and a guest-controlled individual central heating system. Instead
of equipping these new cottages with the same rustic furniture his
other cabins contained, Chandler put in beds with inner-spring
mattresses and decorated each cabin with overstuffed chairs, vanity
dressers, and tables—all made by Simmons, a respected national
furniture manufacturer.

Between 1925 and 1937, Chandler's Tallahassee Auto Court,
which began as a modest roadside camp for motorists, went through
a number of modifications dictated by the demands of motor tourists,
and these changes reflect the influence automobile tourism had on
reshaping the South to conform to different, more modern standards. Chandler's 1937 renovations, however, evidently failed to
bring his facility up to par with tourist courts outside the region,
for as late as the mid-1930s, out of an estimated thirty thousand
motor courts in operation in the United States, the American
Automobile Association found only a small percentage in the South
that it could recommend to its members.[16]

But improvements like those made by Chandler undoubtedly
helped to decrease vacancy rates and attract a wealthier clientele,
as did other enticements such as the sale of groceries, gasoline,
and other automotive necessities. Some camps, especially those in
the warmer climates of the West and South, lured tourists by offer-
ing them the rare opportunity to view "exotic" animals. During
the early 1930s, on U.S. 1, just outside Baxley, Georgia, the Red
Hat Tourist Camp featured a monkey, an alligator, a black bear,

and several ever-popular peacocks. The bear, which had an insatiable taste for soft drinks, was the menagerie's main attraction, and on a good day the camp proprietor sold as many as fifteen cases of drinks to passers-by and camp residents who liked to watch the bear down a soda-pop.[17]

The absence of comfortable tourist facilities in the South and a widely held belief that tourist camps were dirty, offensive places frequented solely by unwashed vagrants led the thousands and thousands of motorists who wandered through the region during the 1920s and 1930s to seek overnight accommodations in numerous renovated inns and countless private homes opened to the public. Commonly found along the early nineteenth-century roads that connected major population centers, roadside inns, or road houses, like the Half-Way House on U.S. 1 about eleven miles south of Richmond, Virginia, had served the needs of stagecoach travelers until the widespread use of railroads put them out of business. Many twentieth-century American motorists, like their nineteenth-century predecessors, swore that when they came into the South, they rediscovered the appreciated American virtues of generosity, grace, and courtesy, and experienced in inns and tourist homes what life was like during antebellum days. One writer, for example, who visited below the Mason-Dixon line in 1925 proclaimed that things were really different there. "The Carolinas and Georgia," he declared, are "more nearly like the Dixieland of the mid-nineteenth century, than is any other part of this country." And "the country adjacent to the Savannah River," he wrote convincingly, " is surely the Dixieland of the storybooks." That same year another writer observed that "all throughout the South . . . newer and better roadside inns are becoming the rule. Many an old plantation home, long closed, is now open and restored to the splendor of its antebellum days, for the benefit of history-loving, luxury-seeking motorists."[18]

If it was southern hospitality that motorists sought, there was always a nearby tourist home. On a motor trip down the Dixie Highway (U.S. 41) in 1931, one motorist recalled asking a police officer to recommend a suitable hotel, only to be overheard by a hospitable southerner who insisted that the tourist stay at his home. "Come with me," the tourist remembered his host saying. "It will be a pleasure to have you with us." The writer continued, "Those are mistaken who say that the old southern hospitality is a thing of the past; that the automobile has killed it. See if you do not find it in evidence as you journey down on Dixie!"[19]

Thousands of motorists thought they found this kind of uncommon hospitality in every southern city and town through which they passed. During the lean years of the 1930s, although some travelers viewed the operation of tourist homes as last-ditch financial efforts on the part of struggling widows and hapless, bankrupt businessmen, tourist homes in the South helped southerners weather the harsh effects of the Depression. Southern municipalities were generally reluctant to adopt restrictive regulations governing the operation of tourist homes, and anyone who owned a house—usually along or within a few blocks of a main tourist highway—and had a spare bedroom or garage apartment could immediately get into business.

All that was necessary was to erect a sign, "Rooms for Tourists—Meals—Baths—Garage," or place an advertisement in a local newspaper, "Tourists Accommodated, 123 Elm Street, $1.00 per night per person." In 1933, a Maryland tourist home association claimed to have twenty-eight hundred members, and that same year in Richmond, Virginia, alone, some one thousand proprietors of tourist homes paid a five-dollar annual licensing fee.[20] For a nominal price—usually a dollar per guest—road-weary tourists could enjoy a home-away-from-home atmosphere not found in more expensive hotels, and certainly not in an autocamp. Gradually tourist homes prevailed over roadside inns and motor camps in the South as the most popular place to stop for the night.

Tourist camps, auto courts, service stations, and private homes open to the public for overnight accommodations were all new to the roadscape in the South during the 1920s and 1930s. They were expressions of the thriving new national car culture and symbolic of the new wave of modernization engulfing the region. That the well-traveled interstate highways leading through the South car-

Marion Post Wolcott made this picture for the Farm Security Administration in the South Carolina Low Country in June 1939. Long before then, however, advertising was as much a part of the roadscape in the South as racial segregation was to overnight accommodations. Courtesy of the Library of Congress.

ried so many potential consumers caused merchants, manufacturers, businessmen, and anyone who offered something for sale to view the road for the first time as a commercial space and not just a corridor connecting one place with another. Since the Civil War, product advertising had heightened consumer demand in the South, as elsewhere, for previously unavailable merchandise, but the roadscape had not yet been commercialized with advertisements. Outdoor advertisements had generally been confined to central business districts or town squares, within view or easy walking distance of railroad depots.

When automobile tourists began rolling into small towns across

Roadside advertising such as this was common on the well-traveled high-ways of the South during the 1930s. This particular billboard was located on U.S. 1 between Baltimore and Washington, D.C., ca. 1939. Courtesy of the Library of Congress.

the South in record numbers during the 1920s, this practice changed. Fresh-produce, souvenir, hot-dog, soft-drink, and ubiquitous barbe-cue stands were the first roadside enterprises to open along the highway. "There are whole flocks of them that have come into be-ing in the last two or three years," reported a writer for the *Motor Camper & Tourist* in 1925, and the greater portion of them have grown out of the wants of the autohobo." By 1927, wayside con-venience vendors were in such numbers nationally that the *Maga-zine of Business* described their presence "along almost every strip of road in the country." In addition to these seasonal roadside en-trepreneurs, other southerners in more established businesses began to call attention to their enterprises by placing all sorts of signs on fence posts, telephone poles, and buildings along the highway. Within a matter of years highways leading through the South, like those in other parts of the nation, had become so littered with advertisements that organizations like the National Council for the Protection of Roadside Beauty emerged to call public attention to the problem.[21] In 1925 Kenneth Roberts recognized the abundance of these advertisements when he wrote that

> in the North one expects to find—as he does find—a plague of sign boards. In the new South, however, which lures tourists with honeyed words and promises of every sort of beauty, the erecting of roadside sign-boards should be viewed with as much disgust and loathing as grapefruit stealing or murder.[22]

As a general rule, the closer motorists came to a town, the more signs and billboards they encountered, but as time passed, roadside advertising was commonplace just about everywhere. In 1925, one writer reported that tourist signs ran "in bunches, mostly outside of small towns, but mainly are encountered on long jumps between towns."[23] Most roadside signs at first advertised either local services like overnight lodging or camping facilities, or local products like homegrown vegetables or fruit. But it was not long before national corporations recognized the practicality of roadside marketing.

At the same time that the South and the nation were being flooded with an unprecedented number of motorized visitors, two state roads leading from Minneapolis, Minnesota—one to Red Wing and the other to Albert Lea—were the original testing grounds for an unprecedented form of product advertising that employed witty verse to catch a passing motorist's eye.

DOES YOUR HUSBAND
  MISBEHAVE
    GRUNT AND GRUMBLE
      RANT AND RAVE
        SHOOT THE BRUTE SOME
          BURMA-SHAVE

was one of the snappy ads used in the South for the first time in 1930 by the Burma-Vita Company of Minneapolis. It was typical of the clever manner in which the company called its product to the attention of the motoring public. By the mid-1930s, Burma-

Shave signs could be found on highways nationwide and helped the Burma-Vita Company become a success despite the Depression.[24]

In addition to the many national companies, like Burma-Vita, that began to advertise their products along the roadside in the South during the 1920s and 1930s were regional corporations like the Coca-Cola Company of Atlanta. One of the most prolific as well as uniquely southern advertisements was the "See Rock City" sign that was painted on the roofs of barns. The practice began in 1936 just outside Chattanooga, Tennessee, on the Dixie Highway (U.S. 41). Garnet Carter, a Chattanooga land developer, had built a three-hundred-acre resort atop Lookout Mountain, complete with a country club, hotel, and popular one-hole miniature golf course. His own home on the mountain was in a ten-acre area of huge rock formations, some as high as a twenty-story building, where water and wind erosion had carved winding corridors through the mountain's sandstone base. On this unusual parcel of land, Carter's wife, Frieda, built the ultimate rock garden, and after the stock market crash of 1929 caused financial problems for his land development business, Carter had a different idea for the site's use. He spent two years re-landscaping the area and improving the original pine-needle trails Mrs. Carter had built. In 1932, he opened the world's most extraordinary rock garden for business. Calling his enterprise "Rock City," he publicized its location by telling farmers that he would paint their barn free if they would agree to allow him to paint "See Rock City" on the roofs. This practice lasted well into the 1950s and proved to be not only a boon to Carter's tourist attraction atop Lookout Mountain but a landmark in American outdoor advertising.[25]

Beside the narrow ribbonlike corridors that guided tourists into and through the South during the 1920s and 1930s, a new subculture emerged. In signs and billboards that advertised products sold throughout the country and in tourist accommodations that catered to tastes and expectations that were not necessarily southern, a trend toward standardization could be found. Gulf Oil filling stations, Burma-Shave ads, and billboards calling motorists' attention to the benefits of Goodyear tires were all a part of this new direction for the South. These were the institutions through which many southerners first experienced the outside world and witnessed the bold new age of modernization as it was ushered in by highway construction and automobility. In its assortment of barbeque and fresh-produce stands, independently owned and operated tourist camps, signs advertising local products and attractions, and livery stables converted to garages, the roadside exhibited certain sectional cultural characteristics as well. The roadscape in the South had become an outward and very visible expression of changing cultural values.

The new car culture as it appeared along the highway, however, extended motorists only a glimpse of what the South was really like. What many travelers experienced when they came into the South were manifestations of this superficiality. But while interstate highways and the availability of automobiles affected this backward South in ways that, as one writer observed, shook established ways of life to their very foundation and "had more economic meaning . . . than all the Civil War generals combined," the impoverished, tumbledown, sharecropper South, as we shall see in the final chapter, continued to be the norm.[26]

The Legacy of
Good Roads Progressivism

With the passage of the Federal Highway Act of 1921, the United States Congress allocated more money to states than ever before for the improvement and maintenance of public roads. Individual states, however, could secure this money only when they matched it with funds of their own, and for this reason, poorer states, like many in the South, were unable to take full advantage of the available federal revenue.

Adding still to the problem was Washington's commitment to pave interstate highways first. Unquestionably, these trunk-line routes had the greatest traffic volume. They were the arteries that shuttled tourists in and out of the South and made it easier for rural southerners who had given up on farming to find employment in nearby cities. And between 1916 and 1920, these well-marked and well-publicized highways that connected the impoverished rural South with the prosperous industrial cities of the North and Midwest also aided many of the estimated 500,000 blacks who left the South to make a better life for themselves. Those who did not go by train fled the overwhelming problems that they faced either by automobile or on foot and, inevitably wanting to avoid the dangerous back roads of unfamiliar parts of the South, took these routes north.

Nevertheless, as a direct result of the federal government's policy of improving trunk-line interstate routes first, the public thoroughfares that comprised the vast majority of the nation's system of public roads were at first virtually ignored. There were, for example, three federal interstate highways that ran north-south through the state of Georgia: the Dixie Highway, Eastern and Western routes (U.S. 41 and 441); the Capital Highway (U.S. 1); and the Atlantic Coastal Highway (U.S. 17). In 1927, shortly after the federal government assigned numerical designations to these highways, only sections of these routes had been paved. Five years later, in 1932, these same highways had been transformed into uniformly paved, all-weather roads. The vast majority of local roads in Georgia's 159 counties, on the other hand, remained unpaved and virtually impassable during rainy months of the year.[1] Washington, in effect, had left rural southerners, who had suffered for decades with horrendous unimproved roads, wondering if they would ever realize the kind of public road network that had been envisioned since the end of the nineteenth century.

A case in point was Harlan County, Kentucky, or "Bloody Harlan" as it was called in the 1920s and 1930s due to its violent labor unrest and a series of "wars" its residents waged with people living in adjacent counties. Located in the mountainous southeastern part of the state, better known today as Appalachia, Harlan Country was about as isolated from the outside world during this time as any community in the country. Beginning in 1920, Harvey S. Firestone, the wealthy Ohio rubber manufacturer, sponsored an annual contest which awarded a full four-year college scholarship to the public school student who wrote the best essay on the importance of improved roads in his or her community. In 1923, the winner was Dorothy Louise Roberts, a high-school senior from Harlan County.

Roberts was no booster of her community and unhesitatingly attributed its shortcomings and chronic backwardness directly to its isolation. She was most concerned about the ignorance of Harlan County citizens. Excessive public drunkenness and wanton displays of violence had resulted in a 1916 homicide rate in Harlan County of 63.5 per 100,000 people, or over 1,200 percent higher than the national average of 5.2 in all of rural America. Roberts wrote that neither the church, with its lay preachers, many of whom had never been outside the county, nor the public school, with a cadre of underpaid and undertrained teachers, had successfully addressed these problems. She was also of the opinion that Harlan County's isolation was responsible for local farmers using antiquated methods and, as a consequence, wresting only a fraction of the wealth that they could from the land.

All of these problems, Roberts maintained, were caused by the condition of roads which were so bad that Harlan County citizens had not yet been exposed to the modernizing forces of the outside world. The roads were so bad in her part of the South, she explained, that when residents wanted to leave, they shipped their cars by freight to Richmond, Virginia, insteading of risking life and limb by driving. "The average car," she wrote, "is a hopeless wreck after one year of steady bumping over ridges and washouts." Her prize-winning conclusion was that

> if it is true that ignorance explains the backwardness of this territory, then both the church and the school are needed to counteract it. Religious and educational work here rise and fall together. Good churches foster good schools. Vigorous churches and centralized schools are impossible in rural sections without good roads. . . . The jitney, auto truck, and family car will be the chariots from heaven, solving our isolation. Good roads will encourage the auto truck, diversity of crops, improved farming methods, cooperative selling, contentment, and an increase in the economic surplus.[2]

Dorothy Roberts's community was not at all atypical of other rural enclaves in the South that remained as isolated in the automobile age by unimproved roads as they had been during the era of horse and buggy. It is interesting to note, too, that Roberts, like her late nineteenth- and early twentieth-century progressive predecessors, still looked to the future for hope of a better life. In other words, by 1923, as far as Harlan County was concerned, good roads progressivism, either as a movement to improve local roads or as an effort to construct long-distance tourist highways, had meant absolutely nothing. The 1920s and years of the Great Depression also brought very little in the way of road improvements to communities in the South like Harlan County.

During this time, however, growing concern over the region's social and economic deficiencies caused road improvements in the South to continue as an important issue. Many people interested in economic recovery from the devastating effects of the Depression pointed to the inequitable way that the federal government, since World War I, had developed the nation's system of public roads, and they demanded that something be done about it. The voices of protest at this time, however, belonged to developers and businessmen and not to the same grassroots contingent of farmers and rural folk who had earlier advocated farm-to-market road improvements. State and local good roads organizations had been extinct in the South for some time; local road building associations representing the interests of construction companies, road building machinery manufacturers, and asphalt and cement companies argued longest and loudest for reform. In 1929 at a convention of the Florida Road Builders Association, for example, a speaker called attention to this problem by stating that

> there is a rising tide of public demand that we supplement our great paved road program with a secondary or farm-road improvement program . . . as to afford quick and substantial relief from the mud burden. If we were to complete every mile of the Federal Aid Highway system it would still leave 93 per cent of our public roads outside the system.[3]

Four years later, the cry for better rural roads was as loud as ever. "In this country we have developed our main lines of travel to a high degree," commented a writer in 1933 for *Better Roads* magazine, one of the many publications of the road building industry in America at this time. "Some of these roads," the writer continued,

> are not utilized to the fullest extent possible because the network of country roads tapping the ultimate resources of traffic has been neglected. These roads should be the first—not the last—concern of the Federal Government in planning a construction program directed toward economic recovery.[4]

In the South the lack of tax revenue to address the overwhelming problem of a road network that was historically the worst in the nation compounded the road improvement problem and left most southerners as mired in mud as their ancestors decades earlier.

Nevertheless, southerners continued to attempt to improve their miserable roads. By 1921 highway departments of each southern state had designated state highway systems and had begun the slow process of making long-overdue improvements. A skeletal network of paved highways in every state had taken shape, but for the most part, hard-surfaced roads were found only around larger metropolitan areas and on the federal routes that crisscrossed the region. Most states in the South built their road networks around county seats, and paved roads at first radiated from these locations like spokes from the center of a wheel. Each year, beginning in 1921,

This rural Virginia road, photographed by Arthur Rothstein for the Farm Security Administration in 1939, typified the conditions most southerners experienced daily well into the twentieth century. Courtesy of the Library of Congress.

southern states managed to increase the number of improved roads in the region. Between 1924 and 1933, Texas and North Carolina led in the number of miles of paved roads. During this ten-year period, Texas paved 3,741 miles of its roads, and North Carolina 2,427. This brought the total number of roads paved in the South between 1924 and 1933 to a meager 16,503, and up until the late 1930s, the problem of impassable roads – especially during winter months – continued to plague the entire region. During the Depression, the federal government created the Civilian Conservation Corps, which put unemployed southerners to work building bridges and improving roads in remote reaches of the South. This, together with efforts by states, resulted in many more miles of road improvements for the region. In 1939, for example, when the Federal Writers' Project compiled its official guide to South Carolina, many roads in that state were reported still to lack permanent paving. But the guidebook did reveal that all of the Palmetto State's forty-six counties were linked by paved roads and that "hardly a place in the State is more than six miles from a hard-surfaced highway."[5]

Clearly then as late as the mid-1930s, good roads progressivism had failed to influence meaningful reforms. Sufficient revenue was still unavailable at either the federal or state and local levels of government to fund appropriate programs. And without money, it was simply impossible to create the network of hard-surfaced roads in the South that for more than three decades advocates claimed would help the region rid itself of many of its stubborn problems. The rhetoric of the mid-1930s sounded much the same as the reform oratory of thirty years earlier. Good roads "are of immense significance in evaluating the social and economic status of farm people, who are dependent largely on the roads for their contact with the rest of the world," read an article in *The Literary Digest* in 1933.[6] Good roads reformers had been sure that better roads in the South would bring about many needed changes, but as with the state and local road improvement programs that they advocated, little, unfortunately, was actually accomplished.

One of the main points progressives had made was that better roads would provide the competition railroads needed to influence a reduction in freight rates. This argument seemed altogether reasonable, because if farmers could ship their produce to market more cheaply over improved farm-to-market roads, they could ignore the railroad. Obviously, by the late 1920s, not enough rural roads were improved to cause any significant rate reduction. What did happen as a direct result of building trunk-line routes instead of farm-to-market roads ultimately proved more beneficial to the railroad than to the farmer.

Mindful of this threat to their profit margins, railroad officials took concerted steps to address the situation. The Good Roads Train that the Southern Railroad sponsored on a trip through the South in 1901–2 was a part of this effort. By the 1920s, when the construction of interstate highways commenced, and when the federal government began to devote more money to building these highways than to subsidizing fixed-rail systems, railroad officials adopted another plan. Instead of laying more expensive track, they made use of the existing roads. Railroad officials dispatched trucks and buses into remote areas of the South not served by rail lines. There, these motor vehicles collected both farm produce and passengers and brought them to the nearest railhead, charging, of course, for the additional service.[7]

Industrial development and educational advancement – the two most sought-after ways in which southerners wanted the South changed – also saw little improvement. In 1929, when Richard W. Edmonds, a member of the editorial staff of the influential *Manufacturers' Record*, visited Atlanta, he commented that although northern industries were interested in looking into the possibility of setting up operations in Georgia, the self-proclaimed "Empire State of the South," little could be expected as long as the roads were so bad. "There cannot be a marked improvement in the industrial situation," he said, "until the state [of Georgia] paves the way for it through construction of standard highways."[8] This was true not only of Georgia but of every southern state. Thus, by 1929 at least, neither the countless campaigns to upgrade state and local roads nor the many efforts to promote and construct long-distance interstate routes had brought the South much closer to its dream of industrialization.

As for educational improvements, there was some definite correlation between the disappearance of one-room schools and the increase in miles of improved roads in southern states. But even this achievement neither raised educational standards very much nor removed entirely the stigma of backwardness. As roads were improved in rural areas of the South, one-room schools there tended to disappear. "Consolidation of one-room country school houses into high grade central schools," according to an article in *The World's Work* in 1922, "is going forward rapidly in [North Carolina]. It would not be possible," the article continued, "without good roads over which the children can be carried in practically all kinds of weather." Ten years later, the American Road Builders Association came to a similar conclusion. "The little red schoolhouse continues its retreat before the motor age," stated an article in *Roads and Streets*, one of the road building industry's trade journals. "Its rate of disappearance," the article continued

> is definitely proportioned to the rate of increase in improved highway mileage. Every acceleration in road construction is marked by a corresponding decrease in the number of one-room schools. School consolidations are continuing to be made at a rate definitely proportioned to the improvements in state highway systems.[9]

Between 1924 and 1930, the year the American Road Builders Association made its study, North Carolina increased its miles of improved roads from 1,714 to 4,025. At the same time, the number of one-room schools declined by almost half, from 2,989 to 1,400. In Alabama, during this same six-year period, good roads increased from 128 to 775 miles, while one-room schools decreased from 3,365 to 2,900. South Carolina saw its improved road mileage grow from 238 to 1,467 miles and its one-room schools drop from 2,561 to 1,600. And in Virginia, as improved roads increased by 850 miles, the number of one-room schools declined by 450.[10]

One-room schools in the South were definitely on the decline, and better roads were given the credit more often than not. But there were not enough improved roads in rural parts of the South at this time to overcome the problem of accessibility that relegated the region to the position of the most backward nationally. The relatively few miles of paved roads that had been constructed in southern states by 1930 had done little to increase the pitifully low percentage of children who attended school in these states or to lower the high rate of illiteracy among southerners. In the South, school attendance in 1930 ranged from 59 to 68 percent of students aged seven to twenty. In northern states, 79 percent of the same age group were enrolled in schools. Furthermore, children growing up in the South in the early 1930s received an average of two years of schooling less than their counterparts elsewhere in the United States. To be sure, child labor in agriculture and industry, as well as a lack of enforcement of compulsory school-attendance laws in the South, were partially responsible for this situation. But when a full 500,000 white school-aged children in the South in 1930 did not have access to a high school of any kind, unimproved roads which made rural schools inaccessible had to bear some of the blame. All of this translated into a high level of illiteracy which in 1930 Professor Edgar W. Knight of the University of North Carolina branded "most conspicuous" because, as he found, it left the region sub-standard and far behind the rest of the nation in educational achievement. "According to the latest published statistics," Knight wrote in *Outlook and Independent* magazine, "the people of at least four southern states have in their garages more automobiles than books in their public libraries; and at least in one of these states the increase in automobiles in the last five years has exceeded the increase in public library books."[11]

Because of the lack of progress made during the 1920s and early 1930s in relieving southerners of the many burdens caused by unpaved and poorly maintained roads, there was an enormous swell of support for road improvements in southern states. This endorsement was far greater than what had been seen during the Progressive Era when good roads in rural communities were the thrust of arguments by southerners who envisioned a more progressive South. And it was this demand, and not progressive reform, that

eventually led to road improvements that reached into the hinter-
lands of the South and provided farmers with the relief they had
sought for so long. What generated this unprecedented outcry for
better roads was not arguments made by good roads advocates but
the widespread acceptance and extensive use of motor vehicles.

Because of the deplorable condition of the region's roads and
the always questionable state of its economy, national automobile
manufacturing corporations at first cautiously marketed their products in the South, and then only in well-populated urban areas
like Atlanta and Birmingham. This prevented southerners from
adopting the automobile as quickly as residents of other parts of
the country. Between 1913 and 1914, the number of motor vehicles
registered in southern states increased significantly. In Georgia the
figure climbed from 12,919 in 1913 to 20,905 in 1914. In the same
one-year period, automobile registration in North Carolina almost
doubled, from 7,710 to 14,719, and similar increases were apparent
in the other southern states.[12]

Over the next few years southerners continued to purchase motor
vehicles enthusiastically, much to the delight of national manufacturers. In 1915, L. L. Stevenson, southeastern sales manager for
the Pullman Motorcar Company, said, "I believe that the south
is now entering upon a great era of prosperity. It is time for the
auto salesman to prepare for the big increase in business that is
sure to follow."[13] The relative prosperity the South experienced
between 1915 and 1919 from the sale of its cotton and turpentine
to northern manufacturers, who supplied not only the federal
government but friendly foreign governments with war materials,
greatly added to the demand for automobiles. This also caused sales
representatives of many national automobile manufacturers headquartered in Atlanta to become even more pleased about future
prospects. In the spring of 1916, K. T. McKinstry of the REO
Motorcar Company reported that "the REO is enjoying the best
demand in the south it has had in ten years. We have sold all the
cars we have," he stated, "and have sold also several carloads which
are yet to be delivered." In 1916, auto sales in the South increased
by 50 percent over the previous year. Northern automobile manu-

facturers sold 59,500 motorcars in Georgia, Florida, Alabama, Tennessee, and the Carolinas alone that year and, within the next two, located 3,240 dealerships in the South.[14]

Demand soon began to outstrip supply, and southern sales agents found themselves trying to fill orders by attempting to obtain vehicles from other sections of the country instead of from besieged, backlogged factories. "The southern farmer," S. E. Ackerman, southern district sales manager for the Franklin Automobile Company, told the Atlanta *Constitution*, "has in a sense suddenly become rich, and of course immediately thinks of a motor car." Another salesman, W. M. Hull of the Franklin Motorcar Company, reported in May 1916 that his company was "enjoying the best demand it had ever experienced in the south," and that he was completely sold out until the coming August. The demand for automobiles was so great in the South that in November 1917 the Atlanta *Constitution* commented:

> Never before have residents below the Mason and Dixon Line been such a factor in the automobile market as they have been this fall, and from the way orders keep coming in from the land of sunshine and cotton, it appears that the winter months also will see a large number of motor cars delivered in that section.[15]

Business was so good that many manufacturers and their representatives were forced to admit that in the past they had not taken the region seriously enough as a marketplace. Perhaps one automobile salesman best summed up the situation when he commented, "In a nutshell, we have not given this section the study we should have given it. We do not realize how the people of the southern states have taken hold of this 'good roads' movement and many of us have lost ground for that very reason." Between 1915 and 1920, the number of motor vehicles registered in the South grew from approximately 25,000 to well over 146,000.[16]

Southerners purchased motor vehicles for many different reasons. Residents of small towns and smaller rural communities took to the automobile in ways manufacturers never dreamed. "Once upon a time, and not so far distant," editorialized the Atlanta *Constitution* in 1912, "the farmer and the automobile were . . . as incompatible as oil and water. But today farmers are among the foremost owners of cars." Whether they could afford one or not, or whether the roads over which they drove were improved or not, by 1920, farmers in the South, as well as other parts of the country, viewed automobiles as desirable additions to their rural livelihood. As Reynold Wik has shown, because of their sturdy construction and low cost, Model T Fords were very popular among farmers. They modified their Tin Lizzies in all sorts of inventive ways to help them more easily accomplish various agricultural chores, including pulling plows, operating corn shellers, powering cotton gins, and generating electricity for barns and farm houses.[17]

Some rural southerners eventually even considered the purchase of an automobile more important than installing indoor plumbing. The idea of being able to escape the isolation of the farm, which accounts for farmers' initial interest in automobiles instead of trucks, was obviously a higher priority than dispensing with the century-old institutions of the well and the outhouse. The status that went along with owning an automobile also motivated some southerners to purchase cars that were less utilitarian and more socially conspicuous than a Model T or a truck. "The number of high-grade, six-cylinder cars that will be found 'three-quartered' toward the sidewalk [in small towns across the South]," commented the *Constitution* in 1917, "proves that the best in automobiling pleasures is none too good for the present-day farmer and his family." Farmers in the South had taken such a liking to automobiles that, in 1916, an agricultural official of the state of Georgia remarked that "the farmer who doesn't own either an automobile or gasoline engine is sadly in the minority in the South. . . . The auto has become a requisite on the farm."[18]

Before northern manufacturers discovered that the South was a fertile marketplace for motor vehicles, automobiles—like automotive parts and accessories—were being sold out of catalogs.[19] Salesmen headquartered in Atlanta, which was the distribution center for dozens of national automobile manufacturers and associated products, traveled the region selling motor vehicles and accessories out of these catalogs to general- and hardware-store owners as well as directly. The sales strategy many relied upon was to demonstrate how useful a motor vehicle could be on a farm. By 1923, when the automobile industry began to take a more specific interest in marketing trucks as well as automobiles in the South, this same sales strategy was employed. "The roads of the South are being developed to such an extent," allowed *Automotive Industries*, a trade journal of the industry, "that it will soon be possible to use trucks in almost any section, with a reasonable degree of efficiency." Nevertheless, because of the still deplorable nature of roads in the South, the editors of the journal were cautious in the type of truck they recommended. The truck they believed best suited for the region was one "of particularly sturdy construction, with considerable power, and at the same time very light, and not built to carry more than a ton and a half or two tons."

The article called on sales representatives to make arrangements for a well-known farmer in their sales territory to demonstrate the work-saving merits of a light truck and to publicize the event to attract the attention of other farmers in the area. A seventy-five-acre farm near Bessemer, Alabama, owned and operated by the Long-Lewis Hardware Company of that city, was a model of this particular sales tactic. According to the man hired by the hardware company to market motor vehicles, the farm's purpose was "to help farmers of Alabama and the neighboring states find the proper machinery for use on their farms."[20] As operations of this sort increased sales in the South, manufacturers opened dealerships in southern towns like Greenville, South Carolina, and Chattanooga, Tennessee, an indication that the South was becoming more consumer-oriented and that southerners were viewing the motor vehicle as an indispensable part of rural as well as urban life.

The demand for better roads, therefore, was directly related to increased automobile ownership in the South. Manufacturers were attracted to the South as a marketplace because of the relative prosperity the region experienced during and after World War I and because men like Asa Rountree and other boosters of the New South convinced them that southern states were making a concerted effort to improve their roads. Where unimproved roads had been once argued to be burdensome to horses and draft animals, the same miserable road conditions also proved hazardous to motor vehicles. In 1929, the cost of operating a light six-cylinder automobile over a road stabilized with gravel or stone was 8.62 cents per mile. Operating the same car on a first-class road paved with cement or asphalt cost 2.37 cents less per mile; and this savings over fifty thousand miles, for example, amounted to $1,185, a substantial amount of money to most southerners.[21]

But the big difference was that automobility enabled farmers to go to town more than once a week, and not have to spend all day doing it. In the absence of road improvements this facet of modernization may have been possible, but for most rural southerners, it was not practical. Automobiles were of little use mired in the mud of an unpaved road or stuck in a roadside ditch, and the cry went up to do something about it. Thus, it was not the progressive arguments employed by reformers that got the South onto hard-surfaced roadways. It was, instead, the widespread ownership of motor vehicles. At one time farmers had viewed vintage automobiles as detrimental to their rural livelihood and adamantly resisted taxation to pay for good roads. But by 1920, they purchased automobiles like any other manufactured product and began adapting them to farm life. It was then that they clamored in earnest for road improvements as a pressing necessity. As Cecil Kenneth Brown in his 1931 study of road building in North Carolina noted, what reformers

> had not accomplished in twenty years of issuing circulars and calling conventions and talking themselves hoarse, this new vehicle [the automobile] with the new motive power was to bring about within a space of time so short as to leave even the most prescient dazed before the spectacle of the meteoric rise of the new means of transport.[22]

Good roads progressivism did little to eradicate the backwardness that the overwhelming number of southerners who resided in towns with populations of twenty-five hundred or less lived with on a daily basis during the 1920s and 1930s. The rural South was still as dilapidated and run-down as ever, and southerners were, on the whole, still more illiterate, more impoverished, and more prone to provincial ways of thinking and behaving than Americans in other parts of the country. On the other hand, due to the construction of interstate highways, much of the South had changed. Certain places within the region had become more accessible, and consequently, certain businesspeople and New South promoters—not all of whom, as we have seen, were southerners—benefited.

Interstate highways brought in new ideas and new products and allowed those who lived relatively near one of these new routes occasion to come in contact with people from different walks of life, in addition to the unprecedented luxury of occasionally being able to escape the constraints of the farm for the excitement of the city. These were, no doubt, significant changes for a region that only a few years earlier was isolated from the rest of the nation and inaccessible to most Americans. But these changes were conservative in nature. They ultimately proved of far greater significance to promoters, members of the business community, and land developers than to the vast majority of southerners. This was not the kind of change that promised to produce the more humane, economically efficient, unified, orderly, and democratic results for the South that reform-minded men and women had in mind. These conservative changes were more in line with business progressivism and were the direct result of the widespread mistaken assumption that the interests of the South and its people would be served best by satisfying the needs of business first.

Highway progressivism fathered these conservative changes, and while what was happening to established ways of life in the South may not have concerned many, an indignant few at least took notice. In his contribution to the now famous series of essays *I'll Take My Stand* (1930), Vanderbilt University Professor Andrew Nelson Lytle wrote that "the good-road programs drive like a flying wedge and split the heart of [southern] provincialism—which prefers religion to science, handicrafts to technology, the inertia of the fields to the acceleration of industry, and leisure to nervous prostration." To Lytle and his intellectual associates, the agrarian order was suddenly being outwardly and unmistakably threatened. Industrialization on the farm, including the purchase and operation of motor vehicles to lighten the day-to-day drudgery of farm life, was ill-advised because the farm, as he said, was not the place to grow wealthy, only to grow corn. He wrote that those who believed that motor vehicles would be of great benefit to farmers were fooling themselves, because most farmers in the South simply could not afford them. Lytle stated that the first thing a farmer did when he came into a little money was to purchase an automobile, and this decision regrettably unleashed a chain of events that often resulted in unemployment and even home-breaking. Because of his attachment to his motor vehicle, "gradually," wrote the Vanderbilt professor, "the farmer becomes more careless of his garden. Each year he cuts down on the meat – the curing takes too much time. He may finally kill only a hog or two, and . . . sells all his cows but one." According to Lytle, "farmers receive few direct profits" from the kind of good roads – arterial highways – that were being built in the South. The real beneficiaries of these highways were asphalt and cement companies, motorcar sales agencies, oil and gasoline companies, contractors, bus lines, and trucking operations. These were the same interests that favored long-distance highways over farm-to-market roads and that stood to gain the most from their construction. To Lytle highways were the malefactors of wealth and the impersonal progenitors of the kind of change that promised to wipe out a way of life endemic to southern agrarianism. In other words, according to the Vanderbilt intellectual, highways had not enhanced rural life or helped to stabilize the traditional values associated with farming. Instead, they had worked to erode them.[23]

So, it is clear that the unwanted South that Lytle and his intellectual colleagues hated – the comfortable, convenient, consumer-oriented South advertised in tourist magazines and on billboards along the road – was the one brought about by interstate highways and the new automobility that car-conscious farmers embraced with such unprecedented eagerness. As roads have improved throughout the course of the twentieth century, the poor, provincial, and dilapidated South, the one that good roads reformers sought to change and the one that Andrew Nelson Lytle saw being exploited by commercial interests, still exists, like no place in the nation, beside the slick, commercial, comfortable South, the one that highway progressivism helped create. This new South, of course, was in the making many decades before the automobile age, but it took the demands of motorized tourists who came south on vacation, the forcefulness of southern business leaders and highway promoters, in addition to the aspirations of a new generation of motorized farmers, to bring it to fruition. Today, as tourists speed south on multilane interstate highways in search of sunshine and recreation at "Sunbelt" resorts like Hilton Head Island off the South Carolina coast and vacation playgrounds like Walt Disney World in central Florida, the old impoverished South seems to receive even less notice than it did when progressive reformers agitated for road improvements as a means of alleviating their misery and relieving the region of the burdens of backwardness. Thus, during the twentieth century, tourist highways and automobility, the very icons of modernization, have been instrumental in the perpetuation of one South and the creation of a second: the first of poverty and the other of promise. And this, as much as anything else, is the legacy of southern progressivism.

Chronology

1885–92	Farmers include road improvements as a part of Populist demands
1893	Office of Road Inquiry created within the U.S. Dept. of Agriculture
1896	Rural Free Delivery of mail inaugurated
1898	North Alabama Good Roads Association organized
1899	Asheville–Buncombe County, North Carolina, Good Road Association organized
1901–2	Good Roads Train tours southern states
1902–8	Automobile speed contests held in Daytona Beach and Ormond Beach, Florida, and Savannah, Georgia
1908	R. H. "Pathfinder" Johnston blazes auto trails between North and South
	John Hollis Bankhead, Sr., assumes duties in U.S. Senate
1909	National Highway between New York City and Atlanta opened
	Capital Highway Association organized
1910	AAA publishes its first official tour guide to the South
1911	Glidden Tour from New York City to Atlanta to Jacksonville, Florida
1912	Good Roads Days practice begins in southern states

1913	United States Good Roads Association organized
	Colleges and universities in the South begin instruction in road improvement science and technology
1914	American Road Congress holds fourth annual convention, in Atlanta
1915	Dixie Highway Association organized
1916	Congress passes first road improvement legislation in over 75 years
	Bankhead National Highway Association organized
1917	By this year, all southern states have highway departments
1918	ACA publishes its "Dixie Tour"
1919	Tin-Can Tourists of America organized in DeSoto Park, Tampa, Florida
1921	Federal Highway Act passed
	Gulf Oil Company opens first gasoline "filling" stations in the South
1922–26	*Saturday Evening Post* articles about Florida appear
1926	Washington federalizes national interstate network of highways

Notes

Introduction

1. Francis B. Simkins, *The Old South and the New: A History, 1820–1947* (New York: Knopf, 1947), 374.
2. Dewey Grantham, *Southern Progressivism: The Reconciliation of Progress and Tradition* (Knoxville: Univ. of Tennessee Press, 1983), xv.

Chapter 1

1. Quoted in North Carolina Geological and Economic Survey, Economic Paper #30, *Proceedings of the North Carolina Good Roads Association* (Raleigh: Edwards and Broughton, 1912), 10–11.
2. Philip Parker Mason, "The League of American Wheelmen and the Good Roads Movement" (Ph.D. diss., Univ. of Michigan, 1957), chaps. 3 and 4, p. 50n.
3. William Faulkner, *The Reivers: A Reminiscence* (New York: Random House, 1962), 84.
4. Statistics cited in Logan Waller Page, "The Necessity of Road Improvements in the South," *South Atlantic Quarterly* 9 (April 1910): 156; R. H. Johnston, "Touring from North to South," *The Travel Magazine* 14 (December 1908): 122.
5. Charles M. Gardner, *The Grange: Friend of the Farmer* (Washington, D.C.: National Grange, 1949), 107.
6. Harry H. Stone, "Good Roads," *Methodist Review* (July–August 1896): 419–21.
7. J. E. Pennybacker, Jr., "The Road Situation in the South," *Southern Good Roads* 1 (January 1910): 9–10.
8. W. H. Hand, "Relation of Good Roads to Schools," unpublished typewritten manuscript, John Hollis Bankhead, Sr., Papers, Alabama Dept. of Archives and History, Montgomery (hereafter cited as JHB Papers); Winston

quoted in Martin Dodge, "Relation of Roads to Rural Population," Bulletin #23, U.S. Dept. of Agriculture, Office of Public Road Inquiries, *Road Conventions in the Southern States, 1901* (Washington: U.S. Government Printing Office, 1902), 13–15.

9. "Improved Roads a Necessity," *Southern Farm Gazette* (May 1909): 1; John W. Abercrombie, "Common Schools as Affected by Roads" in *Road Conditions in Southern States, 1901*, 39–41.

10. Unpublished typewritten copy of speech delivered at Ninth Annual Convention of Southern Appalachian Good Roads Congress, 20 October 1917, at Nashville, Tennessee, Josephine Anderson Pearson Papers, Tennessee State Archives, Nashville.

11. Harry H. Stone, "Country Life and Traveling Libraries," *Methodist Review* (July–August 1901): 576–80.

12. George R. Taylor, *Transportation Revolution, 1815–1860*, vol. 4 of *The Economic History of the United States* (New York: Rinehart, 1951), 21; Wayne Fuller, "Good Roads and Rural Free Delivery of Mail," *Mississippi Valley Historical Review* 42 (June 1955): 67, 71; Liberty Hyde Bailey, Cyclopedia of American Agriculture 4 (New York: Macmillan, 1905–7), 322; Randle Bond Truett, *Trade and Travel Around the Southern Appalachians Before 1830* (Chapel Hill: Univ. of North Carolina Press, 1935), chap. 4; Post Route Map of the State of Georgia and Outline of South Carolina with Adjacent Parts of North Carolina, Tennessee, Alabama, and Florida, U.S. Post Office General's Office, 1 April 1894, Cartographic Archives, National Archives, Washington, D.C.; "Director General Was Once a Country Editor," *The Arizona Digest* 3 (1 April 1922): 6; Cecil Kenneth Brown, *The State Highway System of North Carolina: Its Evolution and Present Status* (Chapel Hill: Univ. of North Carolina Press, 1931), 33.

13. *Congressional Record*, 57th Congress, 1st sess., vol. 35, pt. 3 (Washington: U.S. Government Printing Office, 1902): 2928 and 5147; *Biographical Directory of the American Congress, 1774–1971* (Washington: U.S. Government Printing Office, 1971), 1497 and 1601.

14. Mason, "The League of American Wheelmen," 30–34, 90–92; American Association for Highway Improvement, *The Official Good Roads Yearbook of the United States for 1912* (Washington, D.C. Waverly Press, 1912), 26–172; *The Farmers' Union Guide*, October 1909, unpaginated.

15. N. S. Shaler, "Common Roads," *Scribner's Magazine* 6 (October 1889): 477, quoted in Mason, "The League of American Wheelmen," 32.

16. *Good Roads Yearbook, 1912*, 282–99; W. McK. White, "Louisiana Now Active in Good Roads Work," *American Motorist* 2 (June 1910): 222–23; Atlanta *Constitution*, "Compendium Edition," 23 October 1912; Page, "The Necessity of Road Improvements," 156–60.

17. R. H. Johnston, "Touring from North to South," *The Travel Magazine* 6 (October 1908): 121.

18. "History of Good Roads Days," *The Dixie Home Magazine* 40 (June 1914): 82; North Carolina Geological and Economic Survey, Economic Paper #35, *Good Roads Days, November 5 and 6, 1913* (Raleigh: Edwards and Broughton, 1914), 7–10, 22–23, and 94–97; Brown, *The State Highway System of North Carolina*, 41; Letter, John Asa Rountree to John Hollis Bankhead, Sr., 6 August 1913, JHB Papers; Spencer Miller, Jr., "History of the Modern Highway in the United States," in *Highways in Our National Life: A Symposium*, ed. Jean Labatut and Wheaton J. Lane, (Princeton: Princeton Univ. Press, 1950), 88; "National Good Roads Days Suggested," *Southern Good Roads* 10 (July 1914): 22.

19. *Good Roads Yearbook, 1912,* 27; Brown, *The State Highway System of North Carolina*, 38; *Report of the Fourth National Good Roads Congress, Birmingham, Alabama, May 23–26, 1911,* ed. J. Asa Rountree (Birmingham: Rountree Publishing Co., 1911), 33; Birmingham *Age-Herald,* 14 February 1910; Southern Pines (N.C.) *Tourist,* 31 May 1907.

20. Harry Wilson McKown, "Roads and Reform: The Good Roads Movement in North Carolina, 1885–1921" (M.A. thesis, Univ. of North Carolina, 1972): 13–14; Mason, "The League of American Wheelmen," 184; *Good Roads Yearbook, 1912,* 294–313.

21. Logan Waller Page, "Object Lesson Roads," *Yearbook of the United States Department of Agriculture, 1906* (Washington: U.S. Government Printing Office, 1907), 26.

22. Statistics and quotations about the Good Roads Train can be found in Martin Dodge, ed., *Road Conventions in Southern States, 1901,* Bulletin #23, U.S. Dept. of Agriculture, Office of Public Road Inquiries (Washington: U.S. Government Printing Office, 1902), 41, 57–58; Fuller, "Good Roads and Rural Free Delivery," 70; North Carolina Geological and Economic Survey, Economic Paper #36, *Proceedings of the North Carolina Good Roads Association* (Raleigh: Edwards and Broughton, 1914), 8.

23. *Road Conventions in the Southern States,* 57–58; *The Official Good Roads Yearbook of the United States, 1912,* 89.

24. *The National Cyclopedia of American Biography* 12 (Ann Arbor: Univ. Microfilms, 1967), 493; *Congressional Record,* 53d Congress, 3d sess., vol. 27, pt. 1 (Washington: U.S. Government Printing Office, 1895): 908; *Congressional Record and Appendix,* 54th Congress, 1st sess., vol. 28, pt. 7 (Washington: U.S. Government Printing Office, 1896): 111–12; *Congressional Record,* 56th Congress, 1st sess., vol. 33, pt. 5 (Washington: U.S. Government Printing Office, 1900): 4633; *Congressional Record,* 58th Congress, 2d sess., vol. 38, pt. 1 (Washington: U.S. Government Printing Office, 1904): 746–52.

25. Anne Firor Scott, "A Progressive Wind from the South," *Journal of Southern History* 29 (February 1963): 54, 58–59; Margaret Shirley Koster, "The Congressional Career of John Hollis Bankhead" (M.A. thesis, Univ. of Alabama,

1931): passim; Thomas McAdory Owen, *History of Alabama and Dictionary of Alabama Biography* 3 (Spartanburg, South Carolina: The Reprint Company, 1978), 88, 91, and 92 (reproduced from a 1921 edition in the Tutwiler Collection of Southern History and Literature, Birmingham Public Library, Birmingham, Alabama); A. G. Batchelder, "The Passing of Senator Bankhead," *American Motorist* 12 (April 1920): 17; *The Dixie Manufacturer* 21 (25 October 1906): 1.

26. *Congressional Record*, 60th Congress, 1st sess., vol. 42, pt. 6 (Washington: U.S. Government Printing Office, 1908): 5152-58; Birmingham *Age-Herald*, 15 October 1909.

27. *Congressional Record*, 60th Congress, 2d sess., vol. 43, pt. 3 (Washington: U.S. Government Printing Office, 1909): 2640-42; *Congressional Record*, 61st Congress, 2d sess., vol. 45, pt. 4 (Washington: U.S. Government Printing Office, 1910): 3753; Letter, John Hollis Bankhead, Sr., to John Craft, President of the Alabama Good Roads Association, 24 January 1909, JHB Papers; Bruce E. Seely, "Railroads, Good Roads, and Motor Vehicles," *Railroad History* 155 (Autumn 1986): 38.

28. *Report of the Fourth National Good Roads Congress*, 33-43.

Chapter 2

1. "Atlanta: The Auto Mecca of the South," *Automobile* 21 (4 November 1909): 755-56; Atlanta *Constitution*, 7 November 1909; Maddox quoted in "Atlanta's National Automobile Show Interests the Whole South," *Automobile* 21 (11 November 1909): 817.

2. E. M. Gray, "Leonard Tufts, 1870-1945," unpublished typewritten manuscript, undated, p. 3, Leonard Tufts Papers, Tufts Archives, Given Memorial Library, Pinehurst, N.C. (hereafter cited as LT Papers); New York *Times*, 10 February 1945; Richard Tufts, "The First Seventy-Five Years: A History of the Village of Pinehurst," unpublished typewritten manuscript, undated, p. 8, LT Papers; Olmsted, Olmsted, and Eliot, "General Plan for the Village of Pinehurst," undated, LT Papers; John C. Olmsted, "Report of Visits," 20 June 1895, LT Papers.

3. Gray, "Leonard Tufts," 9-10, 12-13; "The Capital Route from New York to the South," undated, and "The Capital Automobile Route from New York to the South," June 1909, promotional materials in scrapbook entitled "Capital Highway Association," LT Papers.

4. Robert Bruce, "Touring To Dixie," *American Motorist* 2 (December 1910): 536; Columbia (South Carolina) *State*, 8 June 1909; 10 June 1909, 11 June 1909, 12 June 1909, 13 June 1909; Southern Pines (N.C.) *Tourist*, 25 June 1909.

5. Columbia (South Carolina) *State*, 12 June 1909.

6. "All Ready for National Reliability Tour," *American Motorist* 2 (June 1910):

203–5; Paul D. Gray, "Press-On: The 1911 Glidden Tour," *Southern Automotive Journal* 54 (August 1974): 13, 16–18; John Hammond Moore, "The Auto, Jennie Johnson, and The Glidden Tour," *Atlanta Historical Bulletin* 11 (September 1966: 31–45, Batchelder quoted in North Carolina Geological and Economic Survey, Economic Paper #30, *Proceedings of the Annual Convention of the North Carolina Good Roads Association* (Raleigh: Edwards and Broughton, 1912), 50.

7. "A Great Highway Connecting the South with the North and West Needed," *Manufacturers Record* 64 (25 September 1913): 45–46.

8. All quoted in "A North and South Highway," *Manufacturers Record* 64 (2 October 1913): 61–62.

9. Jane Fisher, *Fabulous Hoosier: A Story of American Achievement* (Chicago: Harry Coleman and Company, 1953), 17, 19–31, 46–49, and 82–92; Drake Hokanson, *The Lincoln Highway: Main Street Across America* (Iowa City: Univ. of Iowa Press, 1988), 3–13; "John Stiles Collins," *The National Cyclopedia of American Biography* 21 (New York: James T. White and Company, 1931): 192–93; Eleanor Williams, *Ivan Allen: A Resourceful Citizen* (Atlanta: Allen-Marshall, 1950), 71, Fisher quoted in Charles E. Harner, *Florida's Promoters: The Men Who Made It Big* (Tampa: Trend House, 1973), 60.

10. Atlanta *Constitution*, 10 November 1914; "Noted Atlanta Editor Pays Splendid Tribute to 'Gil,'" *American Motorist* 12 (February 1920): 42; "Dixie Road Breaks Barriers," *Southern Good Roads* 13 (May 1916): 19.

11. Chattanooga *Times*, 4, 8, and 9 April 1915; Hal F. Wiltse, "A Dixie Highway System," *Southern Good Roads* 12 (July 1915): 7–9; Zella Armstrong, *The History of Hamilton County and Chattanooga, Tennessee* 2 (Chattanooga: Lookout, 1940), 243.

12. Chattanooga *Times*, 10, 13, 25, 26, 30 April and 7 May 1915.

13. Chattanooga *Times*, 20, 21, 22, and 23 May 1915; Hal F. Wiltse, "The Dixie Highway," *Southern Goods Roads* 12 (February 1915): 25; John Chapman Hilder, "What The Dixie Highway Is," *Harper's Weekly* 62 (19 February 1916): 190; Polly Redford, *Billion-Dollar Sandbar: A Biography of Miami Beach* (New York: E. P. Dutton, 1970), 91–92.

14. For a description of the celebration of the completion of the highway, see Howard L. Preston, *Automobile Age Atlanta: The Making of a Southern Metropolis, 1900–1935* (Athens: Univ. of Georgia Press, 1979), 146–48; Atlanta *Journal*, 20 October 1929 and 4 November 1929; Records of the Chattanooga Automobile Club, 9 August and 6 September 1917, 10 April 1919, Manuscript Section, Tennessee State Archives, Nashville. In 1917 the Chattanooga Automobile Club purchased a founding membership in the Dixie Highway Association for $1,000.

15. Records of the Chattanooga Automobile Club, 22 November 1917 and 10 April 1919; "Nation Has New Highway Viewpoint," *Dixie Highway* 5 (January

1919): 7, 10; "Senator Bankhead Emphasizes Importance of Road Building Now," *Dixie Highway* 5 (January 1919): 4; W. D. L. Robinson, "Complete the Dixie Highway as a Measure of National Defense," *Manufacturers Record* 71 (7 June 1917): 72–73; "The Dixie Highway as a Military Road," *Dixie Highway* 2 (August 1917): 1–5; "Good Roads Saved France – What of America?" *Dixie Highway* 2 (May 1917): 1–4.

16. Alma Rittenberry, "The Jackson Highway," *Southern Good Roads* 12 (September 1915): 12; "The Jackson Highway," *Southern Good Roads* 13 (April 1916): 11–13; Samuel M. Johnson, "Lee Highway Association: Its First Eight Years and Its Future," unpublished typewritten manuscript, 23 August 1918; Records of the Chattanooga Automobile Club, 1907–1976, Tennessee State Archives, Nashville; Records of the Chattanooga Automobile Club, 9 December 1920; *Views Along the Lee Highway from Washington, D.C. to San Diego, California* (Washington, D.C.: Lee Highway Association, 1923), 1; Maurice O. Eldridge, "Another 'Road of Loving Hearts,'" *American Motorist* 12 (April 1920): 16; "Bankhead Highway Association," *United States Good Roads Bulletin* 1 (November 1916): 2; "1921 Annual Report of the President of the Chattanooga Automobile Club," Records of the Chattanooga Automobile Club, 27 September 1921; "The North and South National Bee Line Highway," *Southern Good Roads* 15 (February 1917): 16–17; National Highways Association, *Good Roads Everywhere* [map] (Washington, D.C.: National Highways Association, 1926); "Map of the Dixie Overland Highway From Savannah, Georgia, to San Diego, California," *Dixie Borderland Highways Association Bulletin* 2 (July 1919): 15; Spartanburg (South Carolina) *Journal*, 11 May 1925; Thomas J. Schlereth, *U.S. 40: A Roadscape of the American Experience* (Indianapolis: Indiana Historical Society, 1985), vii–viii, 86, 90.

17. W. W. Finley, "Good Roads and the Farmer," *Southern Good Roads* 4 (December 1911): 3–4.

18. Letter, C. O. Raine to the officers and members of the Canton, Missouri, Grange, 10 September 1913, JHB Papers; "Good Roads Convention," *Journal of Agriculture and Star Farmer* (17 October 1913): unpaginated.

19. *Journal of the Proceedings of the Forty-Eighth Annual Session of the National Grange* (Concord, New Hampshire: the Rumford Press, 1914), 136–37; Charles M. Gardner, *The Grange: Friend of the Farmer* (Washington, D.C.: National Grange, 1949), 107–9.

20. J. Wayne Flyntt, *Cracker Messiah: Sidney J. Catts of Florida* (Baton Rouge: LSU Press, 1977), 136–39; Victoria H. McDonell, "Rise of the 'Businessman's Politician': The 1924 Florida Gubernatorial Race," *Florida Historical Quarterly* 52 (July 1973): 39–50; Joseph Hyde Pratt, "North Carolina's Interest in the Construction of Public Roads," *Southern Good Roads* 12 (October 1915): 16–18; Harry Wilson McKown, Jr., "Roads and Reform: The Good Roads Movement in North Carolina, 1885–1921" (unpublished M.A. thesis, Univ. of

North Carolina, 1972), passim; Nathaniel F. Magruder, "The Administration of Governor Cameron Morrison of North Carolina, 1921–1925" (unpublished Ph.D. diss., Univ. of North Carolina, 1968): 164, 170–71.

Chapter 3

1. Diary of John Asa Rountree, John Asa Rountree Papers, Archives Division, Birmingham Public Library, Birmingham, Alabama (hereafter cited as JAR Papers); Birmingham *News*, 27 October 1920; "Great Army Convoy Now Traversing Bankhead Highway," *United States Good Roads Bulletin* 8 (June 1920): 5.

2. D. D. Moore, et al., eds., *Men of the South: A Work of the Newspaper Reference Library* (New Orleans: Southern Biographical Association, 1922), 149 and 155; John Knox, *A History of Morgan County Alabama* (Decatur, Alabama: Morgan County Board of Revenue and Control, 1966), 211.

3. *Alabama Enquirer and Morgan County News*, 7 July 1887.

4. William Warren Rogers, *The One-Gallused Rebellion: Agrarianism in Alabama, 1865–1896* (Baton Rouge: LSU Press, 1970), 77; "The Farmers Alliance in Alabama," *Alabama Review* 15 (January 1962): 5.

5. Rogers, *One-Gallused Rebellion*, 10.

6. *Alabama Enquirer*, 29 March 1888, 18 June 1891, 23 July 1891; Sheldon Hackney, *Populism to Progressivism in Alabama* (Princeton: Princeton Univ. Press. 1969), chaps. 5 and 6.

7. *Men of the South*, 155.

8. Birmingham *State-Herald*, 2 December 1896.

9. Hackney, *Populism to Progressivism*, 137–43; Birmingham *Age-Herald*, 10 July 1898.

10. *Men of the South*, 155; Thomas M. Owen, *History of Alabama and Dictionary of Alabama Biography* 3 (Chicago: S. J. Clark, 1921), 91; "Good Roads Department," *Dixie Manufacturer* 24 (25 February 1911): 9.

11. An article on good roads first appeared in *Dixie Home* on 16 July 1897.

12. "The Tennessee to the Gulf State Highway Association," *Dixie Home* 24 (September 1907): 15; "Alabama State Highway," *Dixie Home* 39 (January 1914): 82.

13. "Expressions of the Press," *Dixie Manufacturer* 32 (10 December 1911): 9–10; "National Good Roads Congress," *Dixie Home* 30 (April 1911): 7.

14. "National Good Roads Congress," *Dixie Home* 30 (April 1911): 7; "Good Roads Department," *Dixie Manufacturer* 34 (25 February 1911): 9; *Report of the Fourth National Good Roads Congress, Birmingham, Alabama, May 23–26, 1911*, ed. J. Asa Rountree (Birmingham: Rountree Publishing Co., 1911), 19–20.

15. Letter, J. Asa Rountree to John Hollis Bankhead, Sr., 20 March 1908, JHB Papers.

16. Letter, Bankhead to Rountree, 19 December 1912; Letter, Rountree to Bankhead, 1 March 1913, JHB Papers; Letter, Rountree to Beasley, 1 March 1913, JAR Papers.

17. Letter, Bankhead to Rountree, 4 March 1913, JHB Papers; Letter, Harding and Radcliffe to Bankhead, 18 March 1913, JHB Papers; Letter, Rountree to Bankhead, 18 March 1913, JHB Papers.

18. Letter, Rountree to Bankhead, 18 March 1913, JHB Papers.

19. Birmingham *Age-Herald*, 27 March 1913.

20. Letter, Bankhead to Thomas L. Cannon, 27 August 1913, JHB Papers; Letter, Bankhead to David F. Houston, 15 April 1913, JHB Papers.

21. Letter, Houston to Bankhead, 17 April 1913, JHB Papers.

22. Letter, Bankhead to Houston, 19 April 1913, JHB Papers.

23. Margaret Shirley Koster, "The Congressional Career of John Hollis Bankhead" (M.A. thesis, Univ. of Alabama, 1931): 34–36; Birmingham *Age-Herald*, 26 April 1913.

24. Contract between the United States Good Roads Association and the Conventions Exposition Company, 1 May 1913, JHB Papers; Letter, Rountree to Bankhead, 24 May 1913, JHB Papers; Letter, Rountree to Bankhead, 20 August 1913, JHB Papers.

25. Letter, Bankhead to Rountree, 27 August 1913, JHB Papers; Letter, Bankhead to Cannon, 27 August 1913, JHB Papers; Letter, Rountree to Bankhead, 2 September 1913, JHB Papers.

26. Letter, Rountree to Bankhead, 4 September 1913, JHB Papers; Letter, Bankhead to Rountree, 10 September 1913, JHB Papers; Letter, Rountree to Bankhead, 13 September 1913, JHB Papers.

27. Letter, Rountree to Bankhead, 20 September 1913, JHB Papers; Letter, Bankhead to Cannon, 5 October 1913, JHB Papers; Letter, Bankhead to Rountree, 3 November 1913, JHB Papers.

28. "Good Roads Maxims," *United States Good Roads Bulletin* 1 (July 1916): 4.

29. Letter, Bankhead to Rountree, 2 July 1914, JHB Papers; Letter, Bankhead to Rountree, 20 January 1915, JHB Papers; "Bankhead Highway Association," *United States Good Roads Bulletin* 1 (November 1916): 2; Maurice O. Eldridge, "Another 'Road of Loving Hearts,'" *American Motorist* 12 (April 1920): 16 and 40.

Chapter 4

1. Litchfield (Connecticut) *Enquirer*, 3 and 24 November 1910.

2. C. H. Claudy, "Touring Through War Country," *The Travel Magazine* 13 (February 1908): 238–40, 249; "Automobiling To Old Virginia," *The Travel Magazine* 12 (April 1907): 264–65.

3. "Where Shall I Spend the Winter," *Harper's Weekly* 49 (7 January 1905): 28.

4. "New Automobile Records on the Ormond-Daytona Beach," *Scientific American* 94 (6 February 1904): 119; "Recent Automobile Races at Ormond and Savannah," *Scientific American* 98 (4 April 1908): 244–45; "No More Florida Beach Contests," *The Club Journal* 1 (25 December 1909): 747; Robert Bruce, "Touring To Dixie," *American Motorist* 2 (November 1910): 479–83.

5. Julian K. Quattlebaum, *The Great Savannah Races* (Athens: Univ. of Georgia Press, 1957), 3–7.

6. "Automobiling To Old Virginia," 264.

7. Bruce, "Touring to Dixie," 479.

8. Albert Bushnell Hart, "See America First," *Outlook* 114 (27 December 1916): 933–38; Seymour Cunningham, "Motor Migrants to the Southland," *American Motorist* 3 (March 1911): 153–55; "Dr. Jackson Arrives," *Motor World* 6 (30 July 1903): 658, 659.

9. American Automobile Association, *The Official 1910 Automobile Blue Book: A Touring Guide to the Best and Most Popular Routes in New Jersey, Pennsylvania, and the South* (New York: The Automobile Blue Book Publishing Co., 1910), 701; Bruce, "Touring to Dixie," 479–83.

10. Bruce, "Touring to Dixie," 479–83.

11. R. H. Johnston, "A Winter Tour from New York to Savannah," *The Travel Magazine* 13 (May 1908): 368–70; R. H. Johnston, "Touring from North to South," *The Travel Magazine* 14 (December 1908): 121–23.

12. Atlanta *Journal*, 3 and 4 November 1909; "Atlanta Automobile Week Awakes South," *Automobile* 21 (18 November 1909): 858; Atlanta *Constitution*, 2 November 1909; "Forty-Seven Cars Start for Atlanta," *The Club Journal* 1 (30 October 1909): 622; Bruce, "Touring to Dixie," 479; "The Capital Automobile Route from New York to the South," unpublished, undated manuscript in scrapbook entitled "Capital Highway Association," LT Papers.

13. Cunningham, "Motor Migrants to the Southland," 153–55.

14. Ibid; Columbia (South Carolina) *State*, 13 June 1909.

15. Charleston (South Carolina) *News and Courier*, 20 December 1910.

16. Cunningham, "Motor Migrants to the Southland," 153.

17. Charleston (South Carolina) *News and Courier*, 20 December 1910.

Chapter 5

1. Peter J. Schmitt, *Back To Nature: The Arcadian Myth in Urban America* (New York: Oxford, 1969), chaps. 1 and 2.

2. Whitelaw Reid, *After the War: A Southern Tour* (Cincinnati: Moore, Wilstach and Baldwin, 1866); Ledyard Bill, *A Winter in the South*, 3d ed. (New York: Wood and Holbrook, 1870); Harriet Beecher Stowe, *Palmetto-Leaves* (Boston: James R. Osgood, 1873); Sidney Lanier, *Florida: Its Scenery, Climate and History* (Philadelphia: J. B. Lippincott, 1875); George M. Barbour, *Florida for Tourists, Invalids, and Settlers* (New York: Dodd, Meade, 1882); Charles

Henry Webber, *The Eden of the South* (New York: Leve and Alden, 1883); James W. Davidson, *Florida To-Day* (New York: Appleton, 1889); Henry M. Field, *Bright Skies and Dark Shadows* (New York: Charles Scribner's Sons, 1890); Bradford Torrey, *A Florida Sketch-Book* (Boston: Houghton-Mifflin, 1894).

3. *The Southern States of North America: A Record of Journeys in Louisiana, Texas, The Indian Territory, Missouri, Arkansas, Mississippi, Alabama, Georgia, Florida, South Carolina, North Carolina, Kentucky, Tennessee, Virginia, West Virginia, and Maryland* (London: Blackie and Son, 1875), 325–26, 350, 362, 378, and 441.

4. David Gray, "The Lure of the South," *Collier's Weekly* 46 (11 February 1911): 19.

5. "Motoring Conditions in the South," *Country Life in America* 21 (1 January 1912): 37–38.

6. Louise Closser Hale, *We Discover the Old Dominion* (New York: Dodd, Mead, 1916), 67.

7. J. Leroy Miller, "In the Land of the Realtor," *The Outlook* 142 (23 January 1926): 69–79; George Elliott Cooley, "Touring the Southland," *Outdoors Pictorial* 3 (December 1925–January 1926): 9–12.

8. American Automobile Association, *1910 Automobile Yearbook* 3 (New York: The Automobile Yearbook Publishing Co., 1910), 700.

9. George W. Sutton, Jr., "The South and the Motorist," *Southern Good Roads* 17 (March 1918): 11; *"The Dixie Tour," 1918 Season: Associated Tours Guides* (New York: Automobile Club of America, 1918), 22–24.

10. Crete Hutchinson, "North Carolina's Mecca for Motor Tourists," *American Motorist* 12 (September 1920): 50.

11. Florence M. Pettee, "From the Wintry North to the Palmy South," *Motor Travel* 11 (February 1920): 11; O. M. Wells, "To and Through the Carolinas," *Motor Travel* 12 (December 1920): 14; Henry MacNair, "The Southern Appalachians from a Motor," *Travel* 21 (May 1913): 13–15; Henry MacNair, "Motoring in the Land of Cotton," *Travel* 30 (March 1918): 12–15, 39–40.

12. Elbert Henderson, "Winter Tours in Summer Climes," *Harper's Weekly* 56 (6 January 1912): 12–13; Pettee, "From the Wintry North to the Palmy South," 9.

13. Kenneth Lewis Roberts, *I Wanted To Write* (Garden City: Doubleday, 1949), 150.

14. Kenneth Lewis Roberts, "The Time-Killers," *Saturday Evening Post* 194 (1 April 1922): 6–7, 56, 60; Roberts, "The Sun-Hunters," *Saturday Evening Post* 194 (15 April 1922): 27, 55, 57–58, 61; Roberts, "Tropical Growth," *Saturday Evening Post* 194 (29 April 1922): 77–78, 80, 83, 85; Kenneth Lewis Roberts, *Sun Hunting* (Indianapolis: Bobbs-Merrill, 1922), 111.

15. Kenneth Lewis Roberts, *Sun Hunting*; Roberts, *Florida Loafing* (Indianapolis: Bobbs-Merrill, 1925); Roberts, *Florida* (New York: Harper and Brothers, 1926).

16. Roberts, *Florida*, 28-29.
17. Warren James Belasco, *Americans on the Road: From Autocamp to Motel, 1910-1945* (Cambridge: MIT Press, 1979), chaps. 1, 2, and 3; Roberts, *Sun Hunting*, 75-76, 80-81, 85-86, 88-89, and 109; Letter outlining early history of Tin Can Tourists of the World, Raymond J. and Mary L. Levett to Howard L. Preston, 9 February 1983 (in possession of the author); Billie V. Tracy, "Tin-Can Tourists," unpublished manuscript, Dept. of Archives and History, State of Florida, Tallahassee, undated, unpaginated.
18. Tin Can Tourists by-law quotation in Tin Can Tourists of the World, Inc., *Constitution and By-Laws* (pamphlet in possession of the author), 15; State of Florida, Dept. of Agriculture, Eighteenth Biennial Report, *Florida's Resources and Inducements, 1923-24*, Nathan Mayo, Commissioner of Agriculture (Tallahassee, 1925), 101; Frank Whitman, "Among the Tented Folk of Florida," *The Florida Grower* (5 February 1921), reprinted by Florida Dept. of Agriculture, in *Florida Tourist* 31 (1 October 1921): 16-21; "Automobile Camps in Florida," *Public Works* 52 (29 April 1922): 305; E. L. Filby, "A Municipal Tourist Camp in Florida," *Public Works* 57 (April 1926): 78.
19. Roberts, *Sun Hunting*, 88-89.
20. *Florida's Resources and Inducements, 1923-24*, 101; "Automobile Camps in Florida," 305-6; Filby, "A Municipal Tourist Camp," 78-81.
21. Atlanta *Constitution*, 10 August, 8 September, and 3 December 1918.
22. "The Quest of Winter Ease," *The Literary Digest* 75 (16 December 1922): 46, 48-54, 56-71.
23. O. M. Wells, "Florida: The Land of Sunshine and Flowers," *Motor Travel* 16 (December 1924): 5-9; Forrest Crissey, "Scenery a Cash Crop," *Saturday Evening Post* 198 (12 September 1925): 91.
24. John D. Long, "Facts and Figures of the Motor Camping Movement," *Motor Camper & Tourist* (June 1924): 33; Edna Lynn Simms, "Motor Tours in Sunnyland," *The Hollywood Magazine* 1 (March 1925): 4.
25. Dudley Glass, "Rhymes of the Road," quoted in Simms, "Motor Tours in Sunnyland," 5.
26. C. P. Russell, "The Pneumatic Hegira," *The Outlook* 141 (9 December 1925): 560.
27. Kenneth Lewis Roberts, "Florida Fever," *Saturday Evening Post* 198 (5 December 1925): 7.

Chapter 6

1. Letter, Woodrow Wilson to Samuel M. Johnson, 5 January 1921, quoted in *Views Along the Lee Highway from Washington, D.C. to San Diego, California* (Washington, D.C.: Lee Highway Association, 1923), 1.
2. A. G. Batchelder, "Accelerating Roads Travel in the South," *Southern Good*

Roads 17 (January 1918): 13; George W. Sutton, Jr., "The South and the Motorist," *Southern Good Roads* 17 (March 1918): 11–12; "Southward the Chilly Motorist Wends His Way," *The Literary Digest* 83 (22 November 1924): 56; Truman Pierson, "Mississippi River Scenic Highway," *Motor Camper & Tourist* 1 (December 1924): 420–21; John D. Long, "Old Spanish Trail," *Motor Camper & Tourist* 1 (March 1925): 614–15; John D. Long, "National Dixie Highway," *Motor Camper & Tourist* 1 (April 1925): 682–83; Alma Rittenberry, "The Jackson Highway," *Southern Good Roads* 12 (September 1915): 12; American Automobile Association, "The Mid South," *Official Automobile Blue Book: Standard Touring Guide of America, 28th Year* 4 (New York: Automobile Blue Books, 1928).

3. Thomas J. Schlereth, *U.S. 40: A Roadscape of the American Experience* (Indianapolis: Indiana Historical Society, 1985), vii–viii; *U.S. One: Maine to Florida*, American Guide Series, compiled by Federal Writers' Project of the Works Progress Administration (New York: Modern Age Books, 1938), map and back cover; *The Sandhill Citizen* (Southern Pines, North Carolina), 12 November 1926.

4. *U.S. One*, 211, 225, 246, 266.

5. Spartanburg (South Carolina) *Herald-Journal*, 2 March 1930.

6. John A. Jakle, *The American Small Town: Twentieth-Century Place Images* (Hamden, Connecticut: Shoe String Press, 1982), 155.

7. Frank Whitman, "Among the Tented Folk of Florida," *Florida Grower* (5 February 1921), reprint by Dept. of Agriculture, State of Florida, in *Florida Tourist* 31 (1 October 1921): 16–21.

8. "The Filling Station as General Store," *The Literary Digest* 90 (21 August 1926): 68; Unpublished typewritten manuscript about experiences of G. Everett Millican, employed by Gulf Oil and Refining Company in Atlanta from 1912 to 1965, undated, unpaginated (photocopy in possession of the author).

9. "Southern Hospitality Reigns at Virginia Tourist Camp," *National Petroleum News* 24 (13 July 1932): 36.

10. Described in Millican manuscript, note 8, above.

11. "Money To Be Made: The Oil-Marketing Story," *National Petroleum News* (February 1969): 114–15; "The Filling Station as General Store," 68.

12. "Gulf Refining Company Builds Service Stations In The South," *National Petroleum News* (12 October 1921): 45; Alexander G. Guth, "The Automobile Service Station," *The Architectural Forum* 45 (July 1926): 33–56; Unpublished typewritten manuscript, "Texaco Service Stations: A History," by Kenneth E. McCullam, historian, Texaco, Inc., undated, unpaginated (photocopy in possession of the author).

13. "Chain Stations 25% of Total, Did 33% of Business," *National Petroleum News* 23 (25 November 1931): 62–63.

14. Myron H. Whitney, "Fording the Atlantic Coast," *Outing* 75 (January–February 1920): 231–34, 282–85.

15. Frank E. Brimmer, "'Nickel-and-Dime' Stores of Nomadic America," *Magazine of Business* 52 (August 1927): 151; John D. Long, "Facts and Figures of the Motor Camping Movement," *Motor Camper & Tourist* (June 1924): 33; Jesse F. Steiner, *Americans at Play: Recent Trends in Recreation and Leisure Time Activities* (New York: McGraw-Hill, 1933), 46.

16. Gilbert S. Chandler, "Starting from Scratch and Building a De Lux Motor Court," *Tourist Camp Journal* (November 1937): 5–6.

17. E. L. Barringer, "Highway Cabin Camps," *National Petroleum News* 27 (9 October 1935): 33.

18. Edward F. Ricketts, "Vagabonding Through Dixie," *Travel* 45 (June 1925): 44; *U.S. One*, 203; Vera L. Connolly, "Tourists Accommodated," *The Delineator* 106 (March 1925): 15, 104.

19. John T. Faris, *Roaming American Highways* (New York: Farrar & Rinehart, 1931), 47.

20. "Maryland Tourist Homes Organize," *Hotel World-Review* (21 October 1933): 6. The statistic regarding the operation of tourist homes in Richmond, Virginia, is cited in Warren James Belasco, *Americans on the Road*, 153.

21. Elizabeth B. Lawton, "The Roadside Becomes Important," *Review of Reviews* 90 (October 1934): 66.

22. Kenneth L. Roberts, *Sun Hunting* (Indianapolis: Bobbs-Merrill, 1922), 152.

23. Adelaide Allen Andrews, "The Signs of the Times," *Motor Camper & Tourist* 1 (April 1925): 650.

24. Frank Rowsome, Jr., *The Verse by the Side of the Road: The Story of the Burma-Shave Signs and Jingles* (Brattleboro, Vermont: Stephen Greene Press, 1965), 14, 38, 73.

25. "See Rock City: Vanishing Sign of the Times," Spartanburg (South Carolina) *Herald-Journal*, 4 January 1987; Chester H. Liebs, *From Main Street To Miracle Mile: American Roadside Architecture* (Boston: Little, Brown and Co., 1985), 138–42.

26. Thomas D. Clark, *The Emerging South* (New York: Oxford, 1961), 127.

Chapter 7

1. "State Highway Department of Georgia System of State Roads," *Georgia Highways* (October 1927): 3 and (December 1932): 4.

2. Harry H. Caudill, "Harlan County, Kentucky," *Encyclopedia of Southern Culture* (Chapel Hill: Univ. of North Carolina Press, 1989); "Influence of Highways upon Religious Life," *Review of Reviews* 69 (February 1924): 184–85.

3. "Farm-Service Roads," *Public Works* 60 (July 1929): 281.

4. Quoted in "Better Roads from Farm to Market Sought," *The Literary Digest* 116 (1 July 1933): 23.

5. Department of Commerce, Bureau of Public Roads, *Highway Statistics: Summary to 1955* (Washington: U.S. Government Printing Office, 1957): 82–84; *South Carolina: Guide to the Palmetto State*, American Guide Series (New York: Oxford, 1941), 88.

6. "Better Roads from Farm to Market Sought," 23.

7. "Road Building Instead of Railroad Building," *The Literary Digest* 91 (16 October 1926): 108; Thomas H. MacDonald, "Highways and Railroads," *Scientific American* 146 (April 1932): 222–25.

8. Quoted in Atlanta *Constitution*, 24 May 1929.

9. "Schools and Roads," *The World's Work* 44 (May 1922): 16–17; "One-Room Schools Become Fewer as Improved Roads Increase," *Roads and Streets* 75 (July 1932): 321.

10. Cited in "One-Room Schools Become Fewer as Improved Roads Increase," 321.

11. "Education in the South," *Outlook and Independent* 154 (8 January 1930): 47–49.

12. Statistics cited in "The Automobile in the South," *Southern Good Roads* (April 1915): 19; and "Distribution of American Motor Cars at the End of 1913," *Motor Life* (May 1914): 15. Considering that 122,411 motor vehicles were registered in the state of New York and 94,656 in Illinois at the end of 1913, southern states still lagged far behind in automobile ownership.

13. Quoted in Atlanta *Constitution*, 24 October 1915.

14. Quoted in Atlanta *Constitution*, 28 May 1916; statistics cited in "U.S. Using 5,466,931 Cars and Trucks," *Motor Age* 34 (12 September 1918): 24.

15. Quoted in Atlanta *Constitution*, 15 October 1916, 25 February and 18 November 1917.

16. Atlanta *Constitution*, 16 May 1915; "Motor Vehicles and Highway Development in the South," *Manufacturers Record*, pt. 2 (11 December 1924): 281–82; Peter J. Hugill, "Good Roads and the Automobile in the United States," *Geographical Review* 72 (July 1982): 340.

17. Quoted in Atlanta *Constitution*, 1 April 1912; Reynold Wik, *Henry Ford and Grass-Roots America* (Ann Arbor: Univ. of Michigan Press, 1972), chap. 2.

18. Quoted in Atlanta *Constitution*, 8 April 1917; 24 September and 15 October 1916.

19. Willard Neal, "When Atlanta Got Out and Under," *Atlanta Journal Magazine* (7 July 1946): 8–9.

20. "Time Has Come for Sale of Trucks to Southern Farmers," *Automotive Industries* 48 (15 February 1923): 317–18.

21. Cited in "Georgia Must Pave Its Roads to Attract New Industries," Atlanta *Constitution* (24 May 1929): 3.

22. Cecil Kenneth Brown, *The State Highway System of North Carolina: Its Evolution and Present Status* (Chapel Hill: Univ. of North Carolina Press, 1931), 53.

23. Andrew Nelson Lytle, "The Hind Tit," in *I'll Take My Stand: The South and the Agrarian Tradition* (New York: Harper and Brothers, 1930), 234–40.

Bibliographic Essay

There is a wealth of unmined source material pertaining to road improvement efforts in the American South during the first few decades of the twentieth century. I first became interested in this subject when I was doing the research on my dissertation. As I poured through the Atlanta newspapers in search of evidence pertaining to the automobile's impact on the Georgia capital, I encountered numerous articles about good roads and their value to the uplift of the South. If the attention that road improvements got in newspapers and magazines published throughout the South is any sort of gauge, then the lack of good roads was as much on the minds of southerners at the turn of the century as any other progressive issue.

Anyone interested in the good roads movement should first consult two sources: W. S. Holt, *The Bureau of Public Roads: Its History, Activities and Organization* (Baltimore: Johns Hopkins Univ. Press, 1923), and Philip Parker Mason, *The League of American Wheelmen and the Good-Roads Movement, 1880–1905* (Ann Arbor: Univ. of Michigan Press, 1957). Both provide the background for understanding how the movement evolved in the United States and the role played by the federal government. Wayne Fuller's article "Good Roads and Rural Free Delivery of Mail," *Mississippi Valley Historical Review* 42 (June 1955): 67–83, provides a general understanding of federal good roads legislation during the period prior to the landmark Federal Highway Act of 1916. For a good analysis of the social justification for good roads, see Bruce E. Seely, *Building the American Highway System: Engineers as Policy Makers* (Philadelphia: Temple Univ. Press, 1987). The relationship between American railroads and the good roads movement is explained in Seely's "Railroads,

Good Roads, and Motor Vehicles: Managing Technological Change,"
Railroad History 155 (Autumn 1986): 35–44. F. L. Paxon, "The Highway
Movement, 1916–1935," *American Historical Review* 51 (January 1946):
236–53, is an overview of the highway movement at the federal level.
Several more recent sources that detail the changing values associated
with automobility and road improvements in the United States are War-
ren James Belasco, *Americans on the Road: From Autocamp to Motel*,
1910–1945 (Cambridge, Mass.: MIT Press, 1979); William L. Bowers,
The Country Life Movement in America, 1900–1920 (Port Washington,
N.Y.: Kennikat Press, 1974); Peter J. Schmitt, *Back to Nature: The Arca-
dian Myth in Urban America* (New York, Oxford University Press, 1969);
Joseph Interrante, "The Road to Autopia: The Automobile and the Spatial
Transformation of American Culture" in *The Automobile and American
Culture*, ed. David L. Lewis and Laurence Goldstein (Ann Arbor: Univ.
of Michigan Press, 1980); Norman T. Moline, *Mobility and the Small
Town, 1900–1930*, Dept. of Geography Research Paper No. 132 (Chicago:
Univ. of Chicago, 1971); Reynold Wik, *Henry Ford and Grass-Roots
America* (Ann Arbor: Univ. of Michigan Press, 1972); John B. Rae, *The
Road and the Car in American Life* (Cambridge, Mass.: MIT Press, 1971);
and two of James J. Flink's excellent books, *America Adopts the Automobile,
1895–1910* (Cambridge, Mass.: MIT Press, 1970) and *The Car Culture*
(Cambridge, Mass.: MIT Press, 1975).

Progressive reform in the South, an especially perplexing subject, is
addressed by Dewey Grantham in *Southern Progressivism: The Reconciliation of Progress and Tradition* (Knoxville: Univ. of Tennessee Press, 1983).
Although Grantham's treatment of road reform measures is disappoint-
ing, he puts to rest the question of whether Progresivism was manifest
in the South. The view that this progressive spirit was a direct result of
the agrarian unrest of the late nineteenth century is expressed in both
C. Vann Woodward, *Origins of the New South, 1877–1913* (Baton Rouge:
LSU Press, 1951), and Sheldon Hackney, *Populism to Progressivism in Alabama* (Princeton: Princeton Univ. Press, 1969). George Tindall, *The Emergence of the New South, 1913–1945* (Baton Rouge: LSU Press, 1967), makes
specific mention of the good roads movement in the South and accounts
for some of the highway building campaigns that followed, but like
Grantham, he draws no distinction between the construction of farm-to-
market roads and interstate highways. Several other sources that helped
me to understand the peculiar nature of southern progressivism are Ar-

thur S. Link, "The Progressive Movement in the South," *N.C. Historical Review* 23 (April 1946): 172–95, and Anne Firor Scott, "A Progressive Wind from the South," *Journal of Southern History* 29 (February 1963): 53–70.

There have been only two studies of good roads progressivism in the South, and both are about North Carolina. Harry Wilson McKown's unpublished M.A. thesis, "Roads and Reform: The Good Roads Movement in North Carolina, 1885–1921" (M.A. thesis, Univ. of North Carolina, 1972), focuses on the political and administrative aspects of the good roads movement in the Tarheel State; and Cecil Kenneth Brown's book, *The State Highway System of North Carolina: Its Evolution and Present Status* (Chapel Hill: Univ. of North Carolina Press, 1931) details the evolution of North Carolina's system of highways. Both, regrettably, contain little analysis of the social and cultural impact of road improvements or address the differences between the pre-automobile good roads movement and the later campaign to build interstate tourist highways. John Hammond Moore, *The South Carolina Highway Department, 1917–1987* (Columbia: Univ. of South Carolina Press, 1987), addresses the social upheaval for road improvements in the Palmetto State at the turn of the century. The thrust of Moore's book, however, is the political maneuvering that went into the formulation of state highway policies. The one secondary source that does assess the changes that automobility brought to the South is Thomas D. Clark, *The Emerging South* (New York: Oxford University Press, 1961). In chapter nine, "The Road South," Clark notes the tumultuous changes that took place in the wake of interstate highway construction and automobile tourism.

There is also a wealth of primary source material on good roads progressivism. The best place to begin is in Suitland, Maryland, at the Washington National Records Center, a division of the National Archives. Housed at this facility is Record Group 30, the Records of the Bureau of Public Roads. Contained within this mountain of bureaucratic paperwork are numerous reports and surveys pertaining to the southern states which reflect how retarded road improvements were in the South compared to other parts of the nation. Next to Record Group 30, the most organized and well-maintained primary material is the John Hollis Bankhead, Sr., Papers, Alabama Dept. of Archives and History, Montgomery. Aside from Margaret Shirley Koster, who wrote her master's thesis at the Univ. of Alabama in 1931 on "the Congressional Career of John Hollis Bankhead," no one has yet to undertake a biography of this important turn-of-the-century southern politician, and that is surprising given the condition and volume of available primary data. The Leonard Tufts Papers, Tufts Archives, Given Memorial Library, Pinehurst, North Carolina, contain not only evidence of Leonard Tufts's persistent effort to promote construction of an interstate highway connecting his real estate enterprise with the outside world but information concerning the formation of the Capital Highway Association. The Minutes of the Dixie Highway Association are contained in the Records of the Chattanooga Automobile Club, 1907–1976, Tennessee State Archives, Nashville. Additional information about the Dixie Highway, including several maps detailing the route and construction progress, are in the Josephine Anderson Pearson Papers, also housed at the Tennessee State Archives. The Pearson Papers contain documentation of this early twentieth-century educator's involvement in the good roads movement in the South.

The vast majority of the available source material pertaining to good roads progressivism in the South, unfortunately, is secondary. And researchers should note that, like many other contemporary secondary sources concerning the late nineteenth- and early twentieth-century South, articles and stories about good roads were written, for the most part, not to document but to publicize. Inflated claims and embellishments are as common to these sources as the potholes and quagmires that turn-of-the-century motorists encountered on roads and highways throughout the region. Persistent researchers aware of the drawbacks inherent in this kind of source material, however, can ferret out an abundance of telling quotations, useful statistics, and pertinent information revealing the difference between the rhetoric and realities of the good roads movement in the South.

The three most fruitful of these contemporary secondary sources are the *American Motorist*, monthly publication of the American Automobile Association; *Southern Good Roads*, published each month beginning in 1916 in Lexington, North Carolina, by the North Carolina Good Roads Association, the Southern Appalachian Good Roads Association, and the South Carolina Good Roads Association; and *Dixie Highway*, official organ of the Dixie Highway Association. Men and women who were leaders in the fight for better roads, not only in the South but nationally, routinely published articles in these three periodicals. Some of the articles that I found most useful are W. W. Finley, "Good Roads and the

Farmer," *Southern Good Roads* 4 (December 1911): 3–5; A. G. Batchelder, "Accelerating Roads Travel in the South," *Southern Good Roads* 17 (January 1918): 13; and "The Passing of Senator Bankhead," *American Motorist* 12 (April 1920): 17; "Cause of Good Roads Vital to the South," *Southern Good Roads* 4 (October 1911): 20; George G. Dawe, "The Good Roads Movement throughout the Southern States," *Southern Good Roads* 1 (January 1910): 3–9; Katherine Gould Clemmons, "The Highways of the South," *Southern Good Roads* 17 (March, 1917): 3–5; J. E. Pennybacker, Jr., "The Road Situation in the South," *Southern Good Roads* 1 (January 1910): 9–10; "Noted Atlanta Editor Pays Splendid Tribute to 'Gil,'" *American Motorist* 12 (February 1920): 42; Alma Rittenberry, "The Jackson Highway," *Southern Good Roads* 13 (April 1916): 11–13; Alma Rittenberry, "The Jackson Highway," *Southern Good Roads* 12 (September 1915): 12; H. B. Varner, "Road Improvement in the South," *Southern Good Roads* 16 (November 1917): 8–11; Hal F. Wiltse, "A Dixie Highway System," *Southern Good Roads* 12 (July 1915): 7–9; Truman Pierson, "Mississippi River Scenic Highway," *Motor Camper & Tourist* 1 (December 1924): 420–21; and John D. Long, "National Dixie Highway," *Motor Camper & Tourist* 1 (April 1925): 682–83 and "Old Spanish Trail," *Motor Camper & Tourist* 1 (March 1925): 614–15.

Joseph Hyde Pratt, who served as the geologist in charge of road improvements for North Carolina, wrote a number of articles, and at least one book, about good roads in the South. See his "Good Roads Movement in the South," *Annals of the American Academy* 35 (January 1910): 105–13; "The Construction of Good Roads in the South," *South Atlantic Quarterly* 9 (January 1910): 56–62; and *Highway Work in North Carolina* (Raleigh: E. M. Uzzell and Co., 1912). Pratt also compiled a series of geological and economic surveys that the state of North Carolina published during his tenure. See, for example, North Carolina Geological and Economic Survey, Joseph Hyde Pratt, State Geologist, Economic Paper No. 44, *Highway Work in North Carolina During the Calendar Year Ending December 31, 1914: A Statistical Report* (Raleigh: Edwards and Broughton Printing Co., 1917). This document as well as the others form a cornucopia of statistical information concerning the development of North Carolina's public road system and can be found at the Woodruff Graduate Library, Emory University, Atlanta.

Maurice O. Eldridge, "Progress of Road Building in the United States," *Yearbook of the U.S.D.A., 1899* (Washington: U.S. Government Printing

Office, 1900), accounts for road building in the United States up to the end of the nineteenth century, and *The Official Good Roads Yearbook of the United States for 1912* (Washington, D.C.: Waverly Press, 1912) is a good statistical source for road building campaigns in America prior to the frenzy for interstate highway construction caused by the prospect of automobile tourism. Martin Dodge, ed., *Road Conventions in Southern States*, Bulletin No. 23, Office of Public Road Inquiries, U.S.D.A. (Washington: U.S. Government Printing Office, 1902), contains a history of the 1901-2 Good Roads Train which ran through the southern United States. Additional statistical data regarding road improvements in the southern states can be found in Logan Waller Page, "Object Lesson Roads," *Yearbook of the U.S.D.A., 1906* (Washington: U.S. Government Printing Office, 1907), and "The Necessity of Road Improvement in the South," *South Atlantic Quarterly* 9 (April 1910): 156–60. At the time Page wrote these articles, he was director of the Office of Public Roads within the U.S. Dept. of Agriculture and therefore privy to a vast amount of information.

Any and all of the major newspapers published in the South during the late nineteenth and early twentieth centuries contain articles and stories about road and highway construction. The ones that I used most frequently are the Atlanta *Journal* and *Constitution*, the Birmingham *Age-Herald*, and the Chattanooga *Times*.

If the volume of information concerning the good roads movement in the South is large, even greater is the magnitude of source material pertaining to the automobile and the unprecedented tourism that it generated in the South. When I began the research on this project, I had high hopes of obtaining a first-hand account of an automobile tourist who came into the South during the first two decades of the twentieth century. Surprisingly, I was unable to find anything of this sort. I did correspond with several original Tin-Can Tourists who related some of their experiences in letters to me, but as far as I know, there is no diary or personal journal maintained in a library, museum, or archive that details the experiences of a motorist on the roads of the South during the 1920s or earlier. This, of course, does not mean that such documents do not exist, only that I have been unable to locate them. The closest thing I could find was the article by Seymour Cunningham entitled "Motor Migrants to the Southland: Log of a Trip from Litchfield, Conn., to Charleston, S.C." *American Motorist* 3 (March 1911): 153–55, which I used to write chapter four. Nine years later, in the fall of 1919, O. M.

Wells, chief roadman for the Automobile Club of America (ACA), also reported an automobile excursion he had made into the South. His article is more technical than Cunningham's and is concerned mainly with road conditions, indicating that motorists living in New York City, where the ACA had its headquarters, also contemplated such a trek. See O. M. Wells, "Going South By Motor," *Motor Travel* 11 (October, November, December 1919): 18–19.

Several earlier published accounts of motor trips into the South also exist. C. H. Claudy, "Touring Through War Country," *The Travel Magazine* 13 (February 1908): 238–40, 249, is about a trip in northern Virginia south of the nation's capital. Later in 1908, R. H. "Pathfinder" Johnston published his two articles in the same magazine that helped me to understand how automobile routes linking the South with other parts of the nation were first determined. See R. H. Johnston, "A Winter Tour from New York to Savannah," *The Travel Magazine* 13 (May 1908): 368–70, and "Touring from North to South," *The Travel Magazine* 14 (December 1908): 121–23. For a description of the pathfinding experiences of Arthur L. Westgard in determining the route of the 1911 Glidden tour, consult his book appropriately entitled *Tales of a Pathfinder* (New York: published by the author, 1920); as well as John Hammond Moore, "The Auto, Jennie Johnson, and The Glidden Tour," *Atlanta Historical Bulletin* 11 (September 1966): 31–45; and Paul D. Gray, "Press On: The 1911 Glidden Tour," *Southern Automotive Journal* 54 (August 1974): 13, 16–18. An account of the seventh annual American Automobile Association (AAA) reliability run, which began in Chicago and terminated in Fort Worth, Texas, can be found in "Laying the Route for the Big Tour," *American Motorist* 2 (May 1910): 163–66.

The most informative of the available early published accounts of motoring into the South is Robert Bruce's two-part article entitled "Touring to Dixie," *American Motorist* 2 (November 1910): 479–88, and (December 1910): 535–39. The appearance of these two articles in the *American Motorist* coincided with the publication of the first touring guide to the South by the AAA. See American Automobile Association, *The Official 1910 Automobile Blue Book: A Touring Guide to the Best and Most Popular Routes in New Jersey, Pennsylvania, and the South* (New York: The Automobile Blue Book Publishing Co., 1910). This AAA pamphlet, along with others like it published by the Automobile Club of America (ACA), may be found in the Library of Congress.

Although less descriptive than those previously mentioned, several other articles deserve mention, including William Jarvie, "From Richmond Over Proposed Highway to Florida," *The Club Journal* 2 (28 May 1910): 138–40 and 2 (11 June 1910): 181–85; Osmond L. Barringer, "An Automobile Trip to Blowing Rock [N.C.]," *Country Life in America* 16 (June 1909): 199–200; Joseph Hyde Pratt, "Possible Tours Through North Carolina, *American Motorist* 2 (December 1910): 540–42; E. S. Trippe, "Through the Southern States," *Travel* 18 (January 1912): 59–60; "The Automobile in the South," *Southern Good Roads* 11 (April 1915): 19; Henry MacNair, "The Southern Appalachians from a Motor," *Travel* 21 (May 1913): 13–15; David Gray, "The Lure of the South," *Collier's Weekly* 46 (11 February 1911): 19; Percy H. Whiting, "Motoring Conditions in the South," *Country Life in America* 21 (1 January 1912): 37–38; Egbert Hood, "Historic Virginia by Motor," *Travel* 17 (October 1911): 662–63; Sarah L. Coe, "Motoring the Shenandoah Valley," *Travel* 22 (November 1913): 12–14; Elbert Henderson, "Winter Tours in Summer Climes," *Harper's Weekly* 56 (6 January 1912): 12–13, and Fred J. Wagner, "A Fall Tour in the South," *The House Beautiful* 32 (December 1912): xxx supp. For an understanding of the problems unmarked roads caused early motorists, see Felix I. Koch, "Road Signs and Mile Posts," *Motor Camper & Tourist* 1 (August 1924): 164–65.

During America's involvement in World War I, automobile tourism was somewhat curtailed, and relatively few articles appeared in magazines and journals encouraging the trend. Louise Closser Hale, who wrote a convincing two-part article about her experiences traveling by automobile through Virginia, contributed to this situation. Unlike other contemporary writers, she was critical of the poor condition of the South's roads. See "Virginia: The No-Man's Land for Touring," *Country Life* 31 (April 1917): 49–52 and 32 (May 1917): 62–64. Two associate editors of *Motor Travel*, the official publication of the ACR, wrote a number of syrupy articles about automobile tourism in the South: Edward H. Wakefield, "Winter Touring in Florida," *Motor Travel* 10 (February 1919): 7–11; "Motoring in the Carolinas," *Motor Travel* 10 (December 1918): 6–9; "On Georgian Highways," *Motor Travel* 10 (January 1919): 8–11; and O. M. Wells, "To and Through the Carolinas," *Motor Travel* 12 (December 1920): 14–15. Other articles during this time are Alma Rittenberry, "Every Automobile Club Should Establish Tourist Bureaus," *Southern Good Roads* 16 (August 1917): 10–13; Henry MacNair, "Motoring in the Land of Cotton," *Travel*

30 (March 1918): 12–15, 39–40; and George W. Sutton, Jr., "The South and the Motorist," *Southern Good Roads* 17 (March 1918): 11–12.

With the exception of Warren Belaso's previously mentioned book, *Americans on the Road*, the subject of Tin-Can Tourism has received very little scholarly attention. This is due primarily to a paucity of source material. Because of its straightforward and candid style, the published account of an early automobile trip into the South that I found most informative is Mary Crehore Bedell, *Modern Gipsies: The Story of a Twelve Thousand Mile Motor Camping Trip Encircling the United States* (New York: Brentano's, 1924). Aside from this, anyone interested in the phenomenon of Tin-Can Tourism should first consult Elon Jessup, "The Flight of the Tin-Can Tourists," *The Outlook* 128 (25 May 1921): 166–69; Frank Whitman, "Among the Tented Folk of Florida," *The Florida Grower* (5 February 1921), reprinted in *Florida Tourist* 31 (1 October 1921): 16–21; "Tin Can Tourists Terrifying California," *The Literary Digest* (16 May 1915): 73–75; Jean Campbell, "Tin Can Tourists, Our Modern Gypsies," *Motor Camper & Tourist* 1 (June 1924): 23, 57; and C. G. Elmore, "Tin Can Tourists of the World," *Motor Camper & Tourist* 1 (July 1924): 91. Elmore's article gives a brief history of the organization. Leslie Bray, "The Trail of the Tampans," *Motor Camper & Tourist* 1 (July 1924): 72–74, details the process of outfitting a touring car and deciding on the necessary items the well-equipped tourist should take. It would seem that the Florida State Archives in Tallahassee would have information concerning early motorized tourism to the Sunshine State, but the only worthwhile document concerning Tin-Can Tourism that I found there was an unpublished and undated typewritten manuscript by Billie Vliet Tracy entitled "Tin-Can-Tourists."

There are several published sources that document the cultural changes that tin-canners caused in Florida. Among the best are Kenneth L. Roberts's books, *Sun Hunting* (Indianapolis: Bobbs-Merrill, 1922), *Florida Loafing* (Indianapolis: Bobbs-Merrill, 1925), and *Florida* (New York: Harper and Brothers, 1926). Others that provide information about specific cities and towns in Florida are "Automobile Camps in Florida," *Public Works* 52 (29 April 1922): 305; E. L. Filby, "A Municipal Tourist Camp in Florida," *Public Works* 57 (April 1926): 78; C. P. Russell, "The Pneumatic Hegira," *The Outlook* 141 (9 December 1925): 560; Edna Lynn Simms, "Motor Tours in Sunnyland," *The Hollywood Magazine* 1 (March 1925): 4–8, 38–39; and "Tourists Invading Alligator Land," *Motor Camper & Tourist* 1 (December 1924): 389–91.

Following the war, and especially during the 1920s, travel literature abounds about the South and the feasibility of touring the region by automobile. Myron H. Whitney, "Fording the Atlantic Coast," *Outing* 75 (January–February 1920): 231–34, 282–85, relates the experiences of a motor trip from Ormond Beach, Florida, to Cape Cod, Massachusetts. Even though the author was a hopeless romantic, his tale reflects the hardships an automobile tourist to the South at this time encountered. In 1924, the *American Motorist* devoted its entire October and November issues to the South. Two of the most useful of the articles in these issues are Helen Topping Miller, "On the Trail of Indian Summer," *American Motorist* 16 (October 1924): 14–15, 46, and James W. Brooks, "Southland," *American Motorist* 16 (October 1924): 7–9, 44, 46, 48, 50, 52. Between December 1920 and December 1926, O. M. Wells wrote a series of articles about the South for *Motor Travel*. Although these are anything but objective in their analysis of automobile tourism in the South, they nevertheless contain useful information. Two other articles of this nature are Forrest Crissey, "Scenery a Cash Crop," *Saturday Evening Post* 198 (12 September 1925): 41, 82, 84, 86, 91, and "Where Winter Bids Us Play: Rambles in the South," *The Literary Digest* 107 (20 December 1930): 31–33, 36.

Some of the most informative sources for this period are maps produced by automobile clubs, highway associations, and commercial publishers. The Library of Congress has a number of these, and the ones I found most useful are Automobile Club of America, *The Associated Tours Guide: 1918 Season* (New York: ACA, 1918); T. A. Dunn, *1922 Authentic Roadmap and Tourist Guide of the Bankhead Highway: Washington to San Diego* (Birmingham, Alabama: Bankhead Highway Map Publishing Co., 1921); the series of Rand McNally *Official Auto Trails Maps* concerning the southern United States published between 1924 and 1928; American Automobile Association, "The Mid South," *Official Automobile Blue Book: Standard Touring Guide of America, 28th Year* 4, (New York: Automobile Blue Books, 1928); and Automobile Club of America, *The 1929 Associated Tours Guide* (New York: ACA, 1929).

Documentation for the portion of this book concerning the social and economic changes that automobility caused in the South came in part from many of the articles cited above. There is, however, no particular source that details the cultural metamorphosis that many parts of the region experienced. As a result, I turned to existing publications that address this phenomenon nationally or locally. I am particularly impressed with Thomas J. Schlereth's study of the Lincoln Highway, *U.S. 40: A Roadscape of the American Experience* (Indianapolis: Indiana Historical Society, 1985). Schlereth employs an unconventional approach to historical research, viewing the American highway as "a mammoth outdoor museum of American History." *Minnesota Farmscape: Looking at Change* (St. Paul: Minnesota Historical Society, 1980) takes a similar approach; and Drake Hokanson, *The Lincoln Highway: Main Street Across America* (Iowa City: Univ. of Iowa Press, 1988), is another work concerning the Lincoln Highway employing, however, a more traditional historiographical approach. I found Daniel I. Vieyra's *"Fill'er Up": An Architectural History of America's Gas Stations* (New York: Macmillan Publishing Co., 1979) to be a very detailed and insightful examination of America's most prolific commercial structure. Chester H. Liebs, *Main Street to Miracle Mile* (Boston: Little, Brown and Co., 1985), is very useful in understanding the evolutionary changes along thoroughfares during the motor age, and John A. Jakle, *The Tourist: Travel in Twentieth Century North America* (Lincoln: Univ. of Nebraska Press, 1985) is a good basic source concerning automobile tourism. Finally, I suggest Ashleigh E. Brilliant, "Social Effects of the Automobile in Southern California during the 1920s" (Ph.D. diss., Univ. of California, Berkeley, 1964), as an excellent source for beginning to understand how the automobile changed the roadscape.

Contemporary secondary sources that I recommend are Jesse F. Steiner, *Americans at Play: Recent Trends in Recreation and Leisure Time Activities* (New York: McGraw-Hill, 1933); "Sidewalk Gasoline Pumps Draw Transient Trade," *Automobile* 29 (9 October 1913): 650–54; Adelaide A. Andrews, "The Signs of the Times," *Motor Camper & Tourist* 1 (April 1925): 650–51, 689; Vera L. Connolly, "Tourists Accommodated," *The Delineator* 106 (March 1925): 15, 104; Alexander G. Guth, "The Automobile Service Station," *The Architectural Forum* 45 (July 1926): 33–56; "The Filling Station as General Store," *The Literary Digest* 90 (21 August 1926): 68; Mildred Seydell, "'That Good Gulf,'" *The Open Door* (June 1926): 3–4 (Gulf Oil Co. in-house publication); George Elliott Cooley, "Touring the Southland," *Outdoors Pictorial* 3 (December–January 1925–26): 9–12, 41; Frank E. Brimmer, "Nomadic America's $3,300,000,000 Market," *The Magazine of Business* 52 (July 1927): 19–21, 52; Frank E. Brimmer, "Nomadic America's Changing Spending Habits," *The Magazine of Business* 53 (April 1928): 445–47, 468; and two studies conducted during the Depression under the auspices of the Works Progress Administration. See Federal Writers' Project, American Guide Series, *The Ocean Highway: New Brunswick, New Jersey to Jacksonville, Florida* (New York: Modern Age Books, 1938), and *U.S. One: Maine to Florida* (New York: Modern Age Books, 1938).

Index

Dirt Roads to Dixie was designed by Dariel Mayer, composed by Lithocraft, Inc., and printed and bound by McNaughton & Gunn, Inc. The book is set in Plantin with Hobo used for display and printed on 50-lb. Glatfelter natural.